Read It Again!

Read It Again!

Revisiting Shared Reading

Brenda Parkes

Foreword by Margaret Mooney

Stenhouse Publishers
Portland, Maine

Stenhouse Publishers
www.stenhouse.com

Credits
Pages 19 and 93: Figures 2.1 and 7.1 from N. Lunis, *Investigating Your Backyard.* Copyright © 1999. Reprinted by permission.
Page 20: Figure 2.2 from B. Parkes, *The Royal Dinner.* Copyright © 1990. Reprinted by permission.
Page 22: Figure 2.3 from N. Lunis and N. White, *Bugs All Around.* Copyright © 1999. Reprinted by permission.
Page 31: Figure 3.1 from B. Parkes, *Crunchy Munchy.* Copyright © 1997. Reprinted by permission.
Page 32: Four lines from the poem "Hands, Hands, Hands" from the book by the same name by M. Vaughan. Copyright © 1995. Reprinted by permission.
Pages 41, 52–54: Figures 4.1, 4.2, 4.3, and 4.4 from B. Parkes, *Goodnight, Goodnight.* Copyright © 1989. Reprinted by permission.
Page 77: Figure 6.2 from J. Hillman, *Goldilocks and the Three Bears.* Copyright © 1989. Reprinted by permission.
Page 96: Figure 7.2 from C. Cory, *The Rain Forest.* Copyright © 1998. Reprinted by permission.
Page 98: Figure 7.3 from D. Glover, *Looking at Insects.* Copyright © 1998. Reprinted by permission.
Page 133: Appendix A from B. Parkes, *Who's in the Shed?* Copyright © 1986. Reprinted by permission.

Library of Congress Cataloging-in-Publication Data
Parkes, Brenda.
     Read it again! : revisiting shared reading / Brenda Parkes.
        p. cm.
     Includes bibliographical references.
     ISBN 1-57110-304-X
     1. Reading (Early childhood) 2. Oral reading. 3. Children—Books and reading. I. Title.
LB1139.5.R43 P37 2000
372.4—dc21   00-055648

Cover and interior photographs by Mary Jean Hull

Manufactured in the United States of America on acid-free paper
06 05 04 03 02 01 00 9 8 7 6 5 4 3 2

To my family
For your belief in all I do,
and your love
Thank you

Contents

Foreword

As I read the manuscript for this book, I was reminded of the opportunity I, like thousands of other teachers in New Zealand, had during the late 1970s to participate in ERIC (Early Reading Inservice Course), a series of twelve one-hour sessions exploring components of a balanced reading program for the first three years of school. Attendees worked through the weekly slide and audio tutor program at their own pace, usually in out-of-school hours. Teachers living in rural areas either took the course working by themselves in their own home or by meeting in small groups in a school, while those living in urban areas studied the units at a center, usually in an area set up as a classroom-cum-resource-room. I attended sessions at a center and looked forward to the informal discussion as teachers came and went.

I clearly remember the buzz as one by one we would leave our individual work-stations or "carousels" and gather in the meeting area after viewing and listening to Unit 6, "Shared Book Experience Procedures." The lively pace of the lesson, the children's enthusiastic and spirited participation in the readings, and the teacher's infectious love of books and absolute conviction that every child in that group was, and would continue to be, a reader had rekindled a dimmed light in each of us. We were individually and collectively committed to making our classrooms as alive with readers and books and children's writing and responses to books as that in which we had been immersed in the isolation of a carousel. We had seen children transported into the world, or rather worlds, of readers. We wanted to transport our students into those same exciting worlds. We had been moved into another realm of teaching. The ERIC unit may well have been entitled "Shared Teaching and Learning Experiences" for we had experienced a new level of teaching.

This book kindled the same quickening of ideas and commitment as ERIC had for me those many years ago. To quote from ERIC's Unit 12

(New Zealand Department of Education 1979): "From the most simple point of view, shared book experience is an attempt to adapt the principles of preschool book experience to the classroom, and to refine the procedures to an even more powerful system of learning strategies."

Brenda has refined and extended understandings about shared reading, enabling teachers to draw children into the joys, delights, benefits, and wonders of reading and the printed word. This book anchors shared reading as an essential element within a comprehensive and balanced literacy program. The range of materials and strategies teachers are encouraged to try, extending real and imaginary vistas and competencies within their students, adds new dimensions in both breadth and depth. The book reminds us of the oft-forgotten essential balance of explicit and implicit teaching and practice; of skimming and scanning and sustained detailed reading and viewing; of fiction and nonfiction, each with their own nuances of style and features requiring a twist within the reader; of cooperative and individual effort; of planned and spontaneous teaching and activity; of introducing a book and rereading it until it is a familiar and much-loved friend; and of being comfortable with the known, yet secure in exploring the unknown.

Shared reading offers unlimited opportunities for students to "ring bells in their experience and they think, 'Ah, yes. That's right' because they've previously worked the rhythms of that language into their system" (Unit 12, ERIC).

This book will help educators, whether they be experienced or beginning teachers, administrators, or parents, to "work the rhythms" of thoughtful and thought-provoking teaching into their system and classroom.

Margaret Mooney

Acknowledgments

Many people helped and encouraged me during the development of this book. To each of them, I extend sincere gratitude.

My entire professional career has been centered around children and how they learn literacy, and my first thanks must go to them, for they are my greatest teachers. In particular, I must thank Sarah, whose young voice lies behind the read-aloud data in Chapter 1 and who was also the inspiration for the first shared book I wrote, *Who's in the Shed?* I must also thank Yetta Goodman, Jerome Harste, and Brian Cambourne, who each helped me not only to refine my observations of learners but also to question and understand what I was seeing.

Warm thanks to the administrators, teachers, and children at Davis Street Magnet School in New Haven, Connecticut; Long Beach and Merced School Districts in California; and at Bethune M.E.G.A. Elementary in Texas, all of whom have so generously shared their schools, their classrooms, their teaching and learning, and in many cases their lives with me over the past five years. You have been a joy to work with, and I treasure the personal and professional friendships that have resulted from our work together.

Some special friends also made valuable contributions. Nancy O'Connor gave me the title *Read It Again!*; Susan Avery and Mellissa Alonso reminded me of things I had said in staff development sessions that I had originally overlooked; Mary Jean Hull took the great photographs that appear throughout the book.

To my assistant, Lesley Fawcett, who has lived through every stage of this book, who has responded with grace and unfailing support to the many changes of direction it took, and who by some miracle still works with me, I give my heartfelt thanks.

Thanks also to the reviewers of the manuscript, whose insightful responses refined my thinking and whose positive comments encouraged me to keep writing.

These acknowledgments would not be complete without loving thanks to the members of my family, who are unstinting in their love and support. You are the wind beneath my wings.

Last, but by no means least, I would like to thank my editor, Philippa Stratton, without whose expert guidance, sensitive support, tolerance for traveling authors, and memorable e-mail nudges this book would never have been published.

Shared Reading

At best, such sharing of books provides a way of delighting the child both in the texts and in their own capacity to learn from and about the texts.

Marilyn Adams

As I walk into Ms. Shelley's classroom, I hear a chorus of happy, enthusiastic voices. The class is reading a big book together. "Snip! Snap!" they chant, "And that was the end of the Gingerbread Man!" Ms. Shelley closes the book amid cries of "Read it again, please!" A shared book session is under way.

What Is Shared Reading?

Shared reading is a collaborative learning activity, based on research by Don Holdaway (1979), that emulates and builds from the child's experience with bedtime stories. In early childhood classrooms, it typically involves a teacher and a large group of children sitting closely together to read and rereading in unison carefully selected enlarged texts. Shared reading can also be done effectively with smaller groups.

The first purpose of shared reading is to provide children with an enjoyable reading experience, to introduce them to a variety of authors and illustrators and the ways these communicators craft meaning, and to entice them to want to be readers themselves. The second, equally important, purpose is to teach children systematically and explicitly how to be readers and writers themselves. It is this second purpose that distinguishes shared reading from read-aloud. As Linda Dorn writes, in shared reading "the children actively contribute to the reading with the teacher's guidance. . . .The teacher's support fluctuates in response to her observations of the children's developing control" (Dorn, French, and Jones 1998, p. 32). The teacher consistently models effective reading skills, strategies, and behaviors and engages children in their use.

The language and pictures in shared reading resources provide a rich context for discussion. In addition, the whole, continuous text enables children to see how all aspects of the text work together to contribute to meaning. This gives them many opportunities to join in the reading, and many choices for where and when to do so. For example, the first parts of *The Little Red Hen* that a child consistently recognizes and reads might be the repetitive refrain "Not I" ("'Not I,' barked the dog. 'Not I,' meowed the cat"). This known part of the text will serve as an anchor for the child's increasing exploration and control of content and meaning and the eventual establishment of some decoding skills.

Children enjoy reading a favorite big book in unison.

The large texts used in shared reading make it possible for children to see the print and illustrations and to enjoy and interact with them in a way similar to bedtime stories. During the reading, the teacher not only keeps the focus on meaning and enjoyment but also increasingly draws children's attention to the print and how it works by sliding a pointer beneath the words being read. Poems, nursery rhymes, songs, chants, stories, and informational texts are used to engage children in pleasurable experiences with books and to lay the foundation for reading and writing skills, strategies, and behaviors in a warm and supportive environment that encourages active participation.

Enjoyment of the experience is paramount. As Margaret Mooney (1990) states, "Personal satisfaction from and the enjoyment of the story, as well as the conviction that reading is worthwhile and that it is for them personally, should be the long term effect of any shared book experience" (p. 30).

How Do Bedtime Stories Contribute to Shared Reading?

The benefits of reading to children have been extensively researched in both home and school settings. Research results consistently show that reading to children in their preschool years helps them to become readers themselves.

Case studies (Baghban 1979; Holdaway 1979; Doake 1981) show that children who are frequently read to at home learn book and print conventions and exhibit reading-like behavior. Through repeated, often self-initiated, rereading they use their current knowledge of the world, language, and literacy to reconstruct the text for themselves.

A study of kindergarten children (Sulzby 1985) produced evidence that children move from forming stories in oral language structures to forming them in written language structures. These findings were replicated in other studies as well (for example, Cochran-Smith 1984).

Research into the practice of rereading favorite books, however, provides the most compelling support for the usefulness of reading to children and the role of reading in enhancing the development of children's literacy. Repeated rereadings of the same text by the same participants never turn out the same way (Sulzby 1987; Martinez and Roser 1985; Yaden 1985; Parkes 1990). Over time, as children request and reread favorite books, their questions and comments increase and become more interpretive and evaluative. In addition, they internalize the role of the experienced reader and attempt to read the stories on their own. They internalize the language of the books and incorporate aspects of it into their play and their everyday talk. They playfully substitute meaningful language and experiences of their own for parts of the text, then revert back to the written language in the book. They make connections between the language or illustrations in different books. Research into read-aloud sessions in school settings (Holdaway 1979; Cochran-Smith 1984; Dombey 1983) has found that a significant feature of the experience is the benefit of cooperative negotiation of textual meanings between readers and listeners. In other words, the discussions that continually make connections between print, pictures, and audience are critical.

When I did my initial teacher training in New Zealand, I had the good fortune to have wonderful professors who knew and loved children and knew and loved books. It was a potent combination, one that gave me a lifelong passion for children's books and for finding ways to share them with children.

Reading aloud to children has always been an important part of my teaching day. However, it was not until I did a longitudinal study of what happens when preschoolers are read to in the home that I came to understand fully the layers of meaning and the potential for meaning making that constitute the read-aloud experience. Nor did I fully realize the strength of children's drive to achieve some measure of independence with the books or the network of connections they made as they did so. A close look at some of the data I collected will show what takes place during reading aloud and how children return to the books independently, not only to enjoy them but also to work on their own agenda.

Reading Aloud at Home: A Case Study

Carrying her favorite book, *The Very Hungry Caterpillar* (Carle 1969), two-year-old Sarah climbs onto the sofa beside her mother. "We read? We read Cappa?" she asks.

As her mother reads, Sarah snuggles close, looking at the pictures and listening intently. From time to time she interjects a comment on some aspect of the pictures or the language. Her mother responds to Sarah's overtures.

Mother (*reading*): "In the light of the moon a little egg lay on a leaf."
Sarah (*pointing to illustrations*): Moon. Egg.
Mother (*smiling and pointing*): Yes. There they are. "One Sunday morn-
　　ing the warm sun came out and POP out of the egg came a tiny and
　　very hungry caterpillar."
Sarah: Pop. (*Laughs.*) Cappa.
Mother: Yes. It looks like your caterpillars. (*Sarah has some silkworms.*)

Increasing Involvement with Content and Process

Over subsequent days and weeks, in addition to independently poring
over the book, Sarah makes many requests to "read it again." Sarah's
family continues to read to her, responding to her comments and initiatives and supporting her increasing involvement in the book in a relaxed,
conversational way.

Mother: "One Sunday morning the warm sun came up and—"
Sarah: Pop, tiny hungry caterpillar.
Mother: Yeah.
Sarah: Tiny caterpillar.
Mother: Tiny hungry caterpillar. "He started to look—"
Sarah: Look food.
Mother: Looking for food?
Sarah: Yeah. He look food.
Mother: What do you think he will eat?
Sarah (*laughing*): Cappercakes [patty cakes], ice cream . . .

Within three weeks Sarah dramatically increased her independent
involvement.

Sarah: And Saturday. Saturday morning and cappercake, watermelon,
　　pickle, um . . . ice cream and pickle and salami, lollipop, pie,
　　sausage, cappercake, watermelon, and was sore tummy.
Nanna: I'm sure he was. He'd have had a very sore tummy.
Sarah: And he was all better. Nice green leaf and was all better.
Nanna: Aha.
Sarah: And then was big, fat caterpillar.
Nanna: Wasn't he.
Sarah: And he was come out and pushes him way out and comes out of

coon and he was beautiful butterfly. Fly away and him was beautiful butterfly. (*She flaps her arms like wings.*) That's it! That's it!

Every now and again Sarah would ask to have the whole story read to her. On these occasions she would listen and look intently. These sessions were invariably followed by a spurt of independence with a new part of the text.

Connecting Text to Self

As time goes by, Sarah's involvement with her books takes on deeper meaning. Here she substitutes a recent dinner experience for the words on the final page of Pat Hutchins's *Rosie's Walk* (1968). She is making, in Ellin Keene and Susan Zimmermann's words, "a text-to-self connection" (1997, p. 57).

(The text reads, "And got home in time for dinner.")
Sarah: Rosie went home in time for hamburger and shake. (*Gives her mother an impish grin.*)
Mother: Oh.
Sarah (*laughing*): No. Home in time for dinner.

Connecting Texts to Texts

Sarah also uses the pictures in *Harry the Dirty Dog* (Zion 1956) to retell the story to herself. As she comes to the illustration of Harry crossing over the railway bridge to absorb the soot and grime from the smoke of a passing steam train, she sees a connection to another favorite book, *The Three Billy Goats Gruff* (Smith and Parkes 1988), and incorporates language from that story into her retelling.

Sarah: Him went up the steps, across the bridge. Trippin' and trappin' across the bridge.

Connecting Text Language to Life

The following weekend, Sarah was playing with some friends at a playground. As they all trooped over a wooden bridge she set up a chant of "Trip, trap, trip, trap" and laughingly exclaimed, "We just like billy goats."

From Novice to Teacher

A year later Sarah, who was then almost five, and her two-year-old sister were visiting me, and she requested a story. Among the selections were *The Great Big Enormous Turnip* (Tolstoy 1968) and *Where's Spot?* (Hill 1980). Sarah responded to *Turnip* with joyous familiarity, quickly taking over the reading and adding further dialogue for each character. When we had finished, she began to share *Spot* with her sister.

Sarah: Look, Emmy. Look at the picture. That's Spot. O.K.? Mmm, Spotty. He's looking for his mother.
Emma: Why?
Sarah: 'Cause he likes his mother. See, Emma? (*She points to the illustration.*) He looks for his mother. (*She points to a flap on the page.*) Is she in there? (*She lifts up the flap and looks at the picture.*) No. There's a bear in there. (*She points to the bear.*) Look, Em. A bear. Say "bear."
Emma: Bear.

Sarah continues in this manner for several pages until Emma begins to lose interest.

Sarah: What's this one? (*Lifts the flap.*)
Emma: Don't know.
Sarah: It's not Spot. What is it?
Emma: I don't know.
Sarah: *Think.* What is it? What is it? You've got to *think* when you read, Em!

Sarah had not yet started school, but from her experience with picture storybooks, she was able to assume the role of experienced reader. In addition, she not only understood but could articulate the essence of reading. She knew that reading was a thinking process.

What Does Sarah's Story Tell Us?

The example of Sarah and her preschool reading experiences have much to tell us about children's literacy learning.

At-Home Reading Is Intimate, Focused on Enjoyment and Meaning

The at-home or bedtime story is an intimate, relaxed experience focused firmly on enjoyment and meaning. Through reading and ongoing dialogue, experienced readers help children bridge the language and content of the books and their own language and experience. They create windows of opportunity for children to join in the reading and make positive responses to the children's overtures.

Respecting and Responding to Learners Is Key

Sarah was always treated as a significant partner in the reading experience. Her active and often playful involvement was not only accepted and celebrated but was also used to determine how the book would be shared each time. The books she made her favorites became firmly woven into the fabric of her life (and her family's) through language and play.

The Child Plays an Increasingly Active Role

The data I collected resonated with earlier studies. Reading aloud was shown to be a dynamic experience with the child playing an active, increasingly involved role, negotiating meaning in interplay between themselves, the language and illustrations in the text, and the experienced reader. Sarah used her readers as a scaffold to provide the demonstrations she needed and to build a framework for the story. During the reading, she joined in or took over self-selected parts of the reading, setting her own agenda. As her comprehension of the stories increased, she was able to weave them into her everyday language and life experiences.

Rereading Favorite Books Is Critical

Over time Sarah's interactions with favorite stories underwent many self-initiated changes. No two readings of the same book were ever exactly the same. On each occasion she brought her growing cognitive, linguistic, and social knowledge and experience, as well as different purposes, to the event.

Opportunities to return to favorite books, either with an experienced reader or independently, allowed Sarah time to savor and experiment with the language and illustrations; to see connections between characters, places, and events in the book and in her world; to make connections to other books; to experiment with the language in her own way; and, finally, to make the story her own.

Books Must Be Readily Available

Sarah's books were always available and accessible. This allowed her to revisit them at different times during the day and to concentrate on her current agenda as a developing reader. Sometimes she would focus on a single page, illustration, or refrain. Other times she would retell the story in her own words or a mixture of her own words and those of the story. She read the books to herself and others, and even sometimes to her toys; and she took her books with her when she visited other family members.

Let us sum up the roles of the novice and the experienced reader in the home setting, as seen through the example of Sarah.

The experienced reader:

- enjoyed reading to and with the child and made the experience intimate and pleasurable
- demonstrated how books work
- negotiated meaning by sharing relaxed conversations about the books and by weaving together information contained in the book's language and illustrations with the child's own language knowledge and life experiences
- helped the child by thinking aloud to make connections between what the child currently knew and the characters, objects, and events in the book
- delighted in the child's initiatives and responses and invited active participation by giving her positive feedback
- made good books readily available

The child:

- enjoyed the experience
- established her own favorites
- looked, listened, and responded to self-selected parts of the story

- confirmed her engagement through gesture, body language, and some oral language response
- independently returned to favorite books on many occasions
- helped choose the books
- had easy access to the books for independent use
- focused on meaning
- incorporated the book language and experience into her world by making text-to-life connections and text-to-text connections

The opportunities Sarah had to return to the books over time, both as shared experiences with responsive adults and independently, gave her depth of experience, and helped her begin to generate (in Holdaway's words) "independent behavior which does not depend on an audience of any kind and is therefore self-regulated, self-corrected and self-sustaining" (1979, p. 61). Such behavior lays the foundation for what Marie Clay terms "a self-extending system" (1991, p. 317) and is what shared book experience is ultimately designed to achieve.

Books for Reading Aloud

Reading aloud to children is an essential part of a balanced literacy program and should be done every day.

The following brief bibliography lists books that have memorable language and illustrations and engaging topics that children can understand and relate to. Each invites active involvement during reading and discussion and is ideal for emergent and early readers.

Alborough, J. 1994. *It's the Bear.* Cambridge, MA: Candlewick.
Allen, P. 1990. *Who Sank the Boat?* New York: Putnam.
Armitage, R., and A. Armitage. 1995. *The Lighthouse Keeper's Lunch.* New York: Viking.
Burningham, J. 1990. *Mr. Gumpy's Outing.* New York: Holt.
Campbell, R. 1987. *Dear Zoo.* New York: Puffin.
Carle, E. 1986. *The Secret Birthday Message.* New York: HarperCollins.
———. 1989. *The Very Busy Spider.* New York: Putnam.
Dale, P. 1988. *Ten in Bed.* Cambridge, MA: Candlewick.
Dyer, Jane. 1996. *Animal Crackers: A Delectable Collection of Pictures, Poems, and Lullabies for the Very Young.* New York: Little, Brown.

Eastman, P. 1966. *Are You My Mother?* New York: Beginner Books.

Falwell, C. 1993. *A Feast for Ten.* Boston: Houghton Mifflin.

Fox, M. 1994. *Hattie and the Fox.* New York: Macmillan.

Gag, W. 1977. *Millions of Cats.* New York: Putnam.

Gelman, R. 1993. *More Spaghetti I Say.* New York: Scholastic.

George, J. C. 1997. *Look to the North: A Wolf Pup Diary.* New York: HarperCollins.

Gilman, P. 1993. *Something from Nothing.* New York: Scholastic.

Hutchins, P. 1986. *The Doorbell Rang.* New York: Greenwillow.

———. 1992. *Rosie's Walk.* New York: Macmillan.

Lowry, L. 1995. *Twist with a Burger, Jitter with a Bug.* Boston: Houghton Mifflin.

Marshall, J. 1995. *Look Once, Look Twice.* New York: Ticknor & Fields.

Martin, B., Jr., and J. Archambault. 1989. *Chicka Chicka Boom Boom.* New York: Simon & Schuster.

Moore, I. 1993. *Six Dinner Sid.* New York: Simon & Schuster.

Rathman, P. 1994. *Goodnight Gorilla.* New York: Putnam.

Reiser, L. 1996. *Beach Feet.* New York: Greenwillow.

Rosen, M. 1992. *We're Going on a Bear Hunt.* New York: Macmillan.

Ward, C. 1992. *Cookie's Week.* New York: Putnam.

Williams, S. 1990. *I Went Walking.* San Diego: Harcourt Brace Jovanovich.

Wood, A. 1991. *The Napping House.* San Diego: Harcourt Brace Jovanovich.

Shared Reading in the Classroom: Capturing the Essentials of the Bedtime Story

Capitalizing on the active and social nature of children's learning, early instruction must provide rich demonstrations, interactions and models of literacy in the course of activities that make sense to young children.

IRA and NAEYC joint position statement, 1998

Shared reading builds on the benefits of the bedtime story to provide a solid foundation for reading and writing. At the same time, it fosters a sense of community, as children collaborate to talk, think, listen, and join in the reading.

In order for shared reading to reach its full potential the classroom situation must closely replicate the content and characteristics that make the bedtime story such a powerful precursor to successful reading.

Elements for Success

A number of elements common to the various research studies can help guide the implementation of shared reading in the classroom:

- The experience is intimate and enjoyable.
- A variety of texts are introduced and explored.
- Children actively participate.
- Approximations are celebrated and responded to.
- Participation increases over time.
- Meaning is collaboratively negotiated.
- Favorite texts are repeatedly requested and reread.
- Resources are readily available.
- Children are encouraged to make life-to-text connections.
- Children are encouraged to make text-to-text connections.
- Children are encouraged to internalize process and content.

Creating an Intimate Environment

The first element essential to effective shared reading is the right physical setting. As much as possible, the intimacy of the home situation should be recreated. I like to have a carpeted area or rug where the whole class or group can sit comfortably together and clearly see the big books, posters, and overhead transparencies. I need a chair that is low enough to allow me to develop synergy between myself, the children, and the book through my voice and body language, and help me create a supportive, interactive experience. The physical setting has to become the classroom equivalent of twenty or more children on my lap at one time!

Only when all the children in the group are comfortably seated, able to see the print and pictures and hear the language, and secure enough to take risks can I engage them in thinking and acting like readers as fully and deeply as I want them to.

Selecting a Variety of Texts

The next essential element of a successful shared reading program is to have a carefully chosen selection of material for reading and rereading, including stories, traditional tales, fables, poetry, songs and raps, and nonfiction. The interests, grade level, and ability of the group are paramount factors in choosing texts, as are the teacher's instructional needs. The reading materials must contain print that is big enough for all to see and illustrations that complement and extend the text. They must also have features that allow the children to confidently join in with some parts of the text from the first reading. The content and layout must support the teacher's efforts, and the text must be worth coming back to many times for many purposes and invite collaborative meaning making.

As I think back on the kinds of books the children in my study made their favorites and the shared books the children I work with have loved, I realize that they all have at least some of these features:

- strong story lines grounded in experiences familiar to children
- factual experiences told through clear writing and organization and supported by photographs or realistic pictures
- lively, rhythmical, and uncontrived language
- illustrations that support and extend the text
- many entry points for children to participate through reading and talking
- humor
- action-packed plots
- memorable characters and language
- a satisfying ending

These characteristics guide me in choosing books for shared reading that children are likely to find interesting and that will lead to young readers' engagement, interaction, and active problem solving.

Inviting Active Participation

It is of critical importance to choose the right resources for shared reading. The texts must delight the children, offer many opportunities for active participation, and have sufficient substance to support many rereadings. These characteristics are also true of good bedtime stories.

Teachers can make reading accessible to all by having available a range of carefully selected texts and text types and providing demonstrations of how the texts work, what readers do, and how they do it. Invitations to join in should not interrupt the flow of the story, but are given as part of the interactive experience. I might pause briefly to wonder what will happen next, or pause imperceptibly for children to supply a highly predictable word, or extend an invitation through body language. In these and other ways the children are drawn into increasing participation so that the reading of the text becomes a collaborative effort involving thinking, talking, and reading. And when children are encouraged by the appropriateness of the book and the support and

Two children turn the pages and point to the words as the group reads.

expectation of the teacher and the group, they will become active problem solvers.

By working this way, teachers can make it possible for all children to be involved in shared book reading from the first day of school. Some will talk about the illustrations, some will join in highly predictable parts such as a repetitive chant, some will listen and watch as the teacher points to the words and reads, a few will predict what might happen next, someone can help turn the pages, but *all* will be acting and feeling like readers.

Collaboratively Negotiating Meaning

I am constantly thinking of ways to model and engage the children in collaborative meaning making by linking their prior experience to the language, illustrations, and concepts of the texts. The idea is to encourage the children to get inside the writers' and illustrators' heads. To do this, I frequently wonder out loud about the decisions the authors have made. For example: I wonder what the artist wants us to think when we look at the animals on the cover of this book? What will happen next?

What makes you think that? I wonder why the author uses the words "wishy washy, wishy washy" to describe washing the animals? I wonder what clues the author and illustrators built in for us?

Children should be encouraged to build connections between the texts and their life experiences and between texts and other texts. Following the ideas of Ellin Keene and Susan Zimmermann (1997), they could be asked to visualize places, characters, and events. They should also be encouraged to collaborate as they negotiate meaning. During these activities, teachers should follow the children's lead and explore their thinking.

Revisiting and Rereading Favorite Books

Books used in shared reading should be available for rereading, and the children should have a say in choosing what to read and how to read it.

One of the most significant features of the bedtime story is that children request the same stories over and over again and spend time with them independently as well. With each reading, they confirm what they already know and use that knowledge to fuel deeper explorations. Although rereading favorite books over a long period of time is a critical factor in children's learning, it is often overlooked in shared reading. This is partly a management problem. Books are frequently kept in a central storage area and checked out as needed to ensure their availability for all. However, each classroom does need a core collection of books that can remain in the classroom for the entire school year. If books are available for only a short time, some children will never have the chance to get to know and love them.

Rereading offers benefits to all members of the group. It enables each child to take something unique from the rereading. Many voices joining in unison to read a much-loved book build a momentum that carries readers forward. This in turn creates an environment where children feel safe to take risks, to try things out, and to learn from each other.

The more experienced readers might be able to read the whole text, their familiarity with the content enabling them to focus on fluency and phrasing. Some children may notice individual words. Others may join in on a chant or refrain, some bit of memorable dialogue, or some other repetitive or highly predictable part of the text. A few children may be echo reading, joining in a second behind the others. Some may just listen to the story, not yet able to join in with the reading, but moving to the rhythm of the language as they look at the print and follow the meaning from the pictures. All of this is significant reading behavior.

The opportunity to return to books over and over again with the support of the teacher and classmates allows children to refine their meaning-making strategies and helps them learn to draw on information from a variety of sources. Over time children will build a collection of familiar books that they can read independently and a repertoire of skills and strategies they can use in understanding both familiar and new texts.

Allowing Time for Independent Confirmation and Exploration

It is vitally important that children be given time and opportunity to revisit and reread familiar books in paired and independent situations as well as in the larger group. Independent exploration lets them apply the new skills and knowledge they have learned and allows them to practice and orchestrate behaviors that lead to fluency. As Don Holdaway wrote in 1979:

> The bedtime story should not be separated from the independent, productive behavior that it generates. Such behavior normally engages the infant in extensive, self monitored linguistic behavior for longer periods of time, involving far more intensive language use than is the case with the input activity of listening. (p. 61)

Children should have access to both big books and their small-book counterparts. These they can use for independent reading; for discussion with friends; for independent browsing; as references for retelling and sequencing activities; and for word work, such as identifying high-frequency or rhyming words. In addition, audiotapes of the books can be useful, as children can read and listen along with them. Once the children have had time to explore and become familiar with them, the books can also be used for written responses and for independent work at learning centers.

Essential Tools

A number of tools can facilitate shared reading in the classroom.

A sturdy easel is a must for displaying books securely. Books for shared reading are much too big to be held comfortably, and the teacher should have both hands free to turn pages and to use a pointer and other accessories effectively. You should be free to observe the children and encourage their participation without worrying about whether the book is going to fall over.

Storage areas for books are also needed. They should be kept in a place where they are readily accessible for whole-group sharing as well as small-group or individual use. Some easels have a storage area built into them to contain the books. Another option is to clip the books onto skirt hangers and hang them on a stand, or store them in plastic bags that have a hook to hang them from.

Other essential tools include the following:

- colored translucent highlighter tape
- Wikki Stix™
- Post-it notes of various sizes
- correction tape
- sliding masks
- sentence strips
- pocket charts
- word cards
- magnetic boards
- a white board or chart
- pointers
- magnetic letters
- a plain pointer that does not interfere with the view of the print

Highlighter Tape

See-through highlighter tape comes in many different colors and in two different widths. It can be used to help children identify a variety of language elements, including:

- rhyming words
- known words
- word endings
- transition words
- specialized language
- punctuation
- repetitive text patterns
- capitalization
- letters
- letter clusters
- definitions

Figure 2.1

You can also be a backyard botanist (BOT-uh-nist), a scientist who studies plants. What do plants need to survive? How do seeds grow into plants? A botanist asks these questions and more.

In Figure 2.1, for example, the children have used highlighter tape to identify specialized language.

Highlighter tape is also useful to help children focus on a repetitive example on a page or a double-page spread. In such a situation, children who need a little more time can benefit from peer modeling. For example, consider the repetitive dialogue in the following extract from *Who's in the Shed?* (Parkes 1986).

"It's something big,"
grunted the fat pink pig.
"It's something big."

A more experienced child could find the first dialogue and explain how to identify it, and model how to highlight it with the tape. This type of modeling and demonstration can help a less experienced child.

Highlighter tape is also useful for word work. In the example shown in Figure 2.2 (from *The Royal Dinner,* Parkes 1990), the children have located and highlighted words that have the inflectional ending *-ed*.

So he stirred
and he rolled
and he peeled
and he sliced.
He chipped
and he chopped
and he grated
and he diced.

Figure 2.2

Wikki Stix™

Wikki Stix™ is a product that can be used in a way similar to highlighter tape, but the thin waxed strips are pliable and can be used to circle or underline parts of the text. Wikki Stix™ can be used over and over again. (They must, however, be removed after each use or they will become firmly stuck to the page.)

Wikki Stix™ can be used in an activity such as the following, where the children are asked to identify the words that refer to Jack.

His mother was very, very angry

and Jack was very, very sad.

He went to bed.

When Jack woke up next morning,

the room was dark.

Through the window he could see

a huge stalk and huge leaves.

This activity helps children comprehend the text and draws their attention to syntax. In addition, it provides a powerful model for their own writing.

Post-It Notes

Post-it notes come in a variety of colors, shapes, and sizes. I find them particularly useful when working with nonfiction materials, and children delight in using them.

In the example shown in Figure 2.3, Post-its have been used with an upper elementary group to extend the information in a text by having the children write captions for selected pictures. (The photo is from page 9 of *Bugs All Around,* Lunis and White 1999.)

This next example uses the text in *Bugs All Around* to show how Post-it notes can be used to replace words in a text with words carrying the same meaning.

What Do Bugs Eat?

You can ⬚ bugs closely to see what they eat.

Bugs eat a ⬚ variety of foods.

Figure 2.3

Grasshoppers eat grass and leaves.

Butterflies nectar from flowers.

Correction Tape

Correction tape can be used to cover larger pieces of text for rewriting. I like to use it when I am having the class explore different ways to begin and end a piece of writing. In the following example we are thinking up different ways to begin writing a traditional tale.

In a time long ago

lived a widow and her son, Jack.

They had no money.

They only had a cow.

Sliding Masks

Developed by Don Holdaway (1979), sliding masks are flexible plastic masking devices used to isolate words, parts of words, or letters for detailed observation and discussion. This tool has an advantage over highlighter tape in that the plastic completely conceals the other parts of the word, effectively focusing students' attention on the discussion point and allowing the teacher to progressively reveal the remainder of the word as needed.

In the following example, the group is working with a text in which a word has been covered up. After predicting a word that makes sense in context, the actual word is progressively exposed to confirm the prediction or to allow for self-correction using the revealed information.

The king was de⎿⎽⎽⎽⎽⎽⏌ when he saw the gold.

Sentence Strips

Sentence strips can be used to draw children's attention to visual features of text in a one-to-one matching activity. Books that have repetitive lines of print on the same or facing pages support this modeling activity well.

Working with the text *Who's in the Shed?* (Parkes 1986), the teacher introduces the activity by showing the front cover and having the children recall some of the animals in the story and what they said and did. He then opens the book, and they read the double-page spread featuring the cow.

"My turn now,"
mooed the sleek brown cow.
"My turn now."

Next the teacher displays a sentence strip matching the line "My turn now," and using a think-aloud strategy models how he has determined what line of print the strip matches. "I noticed that the first word began with an uppercase *M*. That matched my strip. Then I saw the speech marks around 'My turn now.' My strip has these marks too."

The strip is held directly beneath the matching line of print so the children can see that the words match one-to-one and can notice visual clues in the letters and the punctuation that help them confirm that the print is the same.

"My turn now."
⎿ "My turn now." ⏌

The teacher then asks the children how else they could tell if he was right. They identify other features of print and punctuation before he moves the strip to cover the existing text. Next he distributes other sentence strips and asks, "Who has the next line?"

As each child holds his or her strip beneath the matching text and validates the choice, the teacher asks the other children, "Is there another way you can check to be sure?" When the matching is completed they read the page again. This attention to visual features of text in context provides children with valuable strategies to apply when checking and self-correcting their reading.

Pocket Charts

An extension of the matching strip activity is to have children rebuild the text of a familiar story in a pocket chart. Here the purpose is to have them maintain meaning through semantic and syntactic information as the text is rebuilt. As each of the children adds a strip they give reasons why it follows the preceding strip. As the text grows, the children reread it to predict what comes next and why, so that everyone in the group is involved in predicting, checking, and confirming.

A further adaptation can be made by assembling the strips in order and covering a number of key words. The teacher supplies the missing words on individual cards and has the children read the text, using semantic and syntactic information to justify why their words fill the spaces.

In each of these examples children work with continuous text and are able to check and confirm or self-correct their predictions across meaning, structure, and visual cues. They are learning to orchestrate multiple sources of information.

White Boards and Chart Paper

I never do shared reading without either a white board or chart paper, or both, close at hand. They allow for an instant response when a child's spontaneous observation of some feature in the book provides a teachable moment. The chart paper allows for a permanent record of some of these instances and can be used on a "reading wall" for the children to refer to for reading and writing.

Using Shared Reading for Implicit and Explicit Instruction

Teachers serve as guides so that children know how to engage in purposeful self direction.

Billie Askew and Irene Fountas

One of the major goals of shared reading is to help children develop a range of effective strategies for reading and understanding text. In Marie Clay's (1991) words:

In order to read with understanding we call up and use a repertoire of strategies acting upon stores of knowledge to extract messages from print. Reading and writing acquisition involves the active construction of that repertoire, with comprehending having a central role...learning of this kind depends upon children being active processors of printed information and constructive learners. (p. 326)

A great deal of teaching and learning happens every time active learners meet with a responsive teacher to read and reread shared books and to engage in discussion and analysis of texts. With ongoing assessment and the goals of the classroom literacy program in mind, teachers implicitly and explicitly model reading and writing behaviors, skills, and strategies.

They carefully structure situations to engage children in problem solving on continuous text as they work through the recursive cycle of reading *to* and *with* the children, and encouraging reading *by* them. Each time this is done, children learn about:

- book and print conventions (through the talk that accompanies choosing a book, looking at the cover, reading the title, talking about the pictures, turning the pages, noticing letters, and identifying words)
- punctuation
- phonemes
- letter and letter sound relationships
- words
- syntax (as it is modeled)
- semantics (as it is used to predict)
- how readers read (as it is modeled)
- the joy and enlightenment that come from reading

Shared resources should be selected carefully to teach specific skills and strategies in reading and writing. Each book may be used in many different ways over a long period of time depending on the needs of the children and the teacher's purpose. Many examples of outlining different ways to use books are given in Chapters 4 and 7.

Any one book should not be overused in a short period of time for every possible teaching feature. Instead, it is more effective to use different titles for different purposes, finding books that provide just the right features for teaching at any given time, just as teachers carefully match books to readers for guided reading.

Shared reading is an ideal way to demonstrate how the three language-based sources of information—semantics, syntax, and graphophonics—work and engage children in their use. The overall goal is to teach children to orchestrate these sources of information.

Semantic Information

Semantics relates to the meaning system of language. Meaning is obtained from the reader's background knowledge and experience and his or her understanding of particular concepts. Semantic knowledge allows readers to build networks they can use to figure out new information in texts and mentally organize it into long-term memory.

Meaning does not exist in individual words. Specific words have meaning only when they are embedded in language. One of the major benefits of shared book reading is that it gives the reader a complete text to work with. The reader can draw on the surrounding text to cross-check information from multiple sources and to monitor that what he or she is reading makes sense.

Ways of using semantic information are continuously modeled throughout any shared reading experience. Children are implicitly involved in meaning making as they:

- look at book covers and predict content based on information in the title and illustrations
- link prior knowledge and experience to the text
- notice details in illustrations
- make connections between books
- predict what will happen next
- visualize and discuss settings, characters, and events

Explicit mini-lessons can be used to focus children's attention on semantic information.

In the following example the semantic knowledge of a group of kindergarteners is developed through use of the text *Who's in the Shed?* (Parkes 1986). The front cover features a cameo picture of a startled-looking group of farm animals. The story centers around predicting who is in the shed from the cumulative picture clues each animal sees as they peep through cutouts in the book that represent holes in the shed. The teacher's introduction has to establish who the characters are, how they feel, and why.

Teacher (*pointing to the illustration*): What farm animals do you see here?
Sarah: A cow.
James: And a pig.
Joshua: There's a lamb too.
Teacher: It could be. What other word could we use?
Megan: Sheep. It's a sheep.
Teacher: We'll have to check the print when we read it and see which one it is.

Sarah: Look at the big horse.

James (*pointing*): That one's a chicken.

Teacher: Could it be anything else?

Sarah: A hen. Maybe it's a hen.

Teacher (*pointing to each one in turn*): Tell me the names again and the sounds each animal makes.

The children happily oblige, mooing and baaing with gusto.

Teacher: Now let's look at the animals' eyes. What do you think the illustrator wants us to notice?

James: They look scared.

Joshua: Yeah. They look frightened.

Teacher: Let's read the title and see if it helps us know why they are scared. *Who's in the Shed?*

Reagan: Maybe there's something scary in the shed. A ghost, like at Halloween.

Sam: Or a big rat.

Teacher: It could be. Let's read the first pages and see what clues we get. (*Reads.*)
"Down at the farm
one Saturday night
the animals woke
with a terrible fright.
There was howling
and growling
and roaring
and clawing . . ."
What could be making those noises in the shed? Do you still think it's a ghost, Reagan?

Reagan: A wolf.

Joshua: Or maybe a dog.

Teacher: Let's read and find out. You join in wherever you can.

This introduction has provided a network of clues to help the children predict and confirm the story as it unfolds. The teacher has helped the children identify the characters and the sounds they make, shown how the cover, illustrations, and title combine to convey information, and demonstrated how readers think. This effective introduction to the book has given the children a powerful set of semantic information, which in turn will support syntax and graphophonic information.

Syntactic, or Structural, Information

Syntactic, or structural, information comes from knowing the grammar or the ongoing flow of language. Readers use the knowledge of grammar they internalized when they learned to talk in order to predict what words are likely to appear next.

Syntactic information is modeled implicitly each time the group engages in reading. Children are immersed in authentic demonstrations of the sounds and patterns of language as they:

- read and enjoy the rhythms of songs, raps, and chants
- listen and join in with narrative and nonfiction texts
- participate in oral cloze by predicting words, story beginnings, and phrases
- take over the reading of repetitive language

In this example of an explicit syntactic lesson, the teacher, Ms. Arnold, has covered selected words in *The Fox and the Little Red Hen* (Parkes 1989) with Post-it notes to make a cloze exercise that focuses on using structure clues.

Fox made Little Red Hen so dizzy
that ☐ fell from the rafters.
Quickly he stuffed her into ☐ bag
and set off ☐ home.

Ms. Arnold: First I want you to read this to yourself silently and put words in the spaces that sound right to you.
Pearce: *She* goes in the first one.
Ms. Arnold: What helps you to think that?
Pearce: The little red hen's a girl—a she.
Ms. Arnold: Who thinks it's something else?
Marilyn: It could be *her*.
Ms. Arnold: Let's read it both ways. Listen and see which way we say it…

Pearce: *Her* sounds wrong. It must be *she*.

Marilyn: The next one must be *his* because it's talking about the fox.

Ms. Arnold: How did you figure that out?

Marilyn: See (*pointing and reading*), *he* stuffed her into *his* bag. The fox is a boy.

Ms. Arnold: Let's read it. How else will we know it's right?

James: It will sound O.K.

Graphophonic Information

Graphophonic information refers to the letter-sound system of language, the relationship between oral language and its graphic symbols. Graphophonic information draws on two sources of information: the phonological system and the orthographic system. The phonological system is concerned with the sounds of language and includes phonemic awareness, which is the ability to hear sounds in words and to identify particular sounds. The orthographic system has to do with how written language is constructed. It includes graphemes, the letters used to represent sounds.

The ability to use graphophonic information is an important part of learning to read. The shared reading of songs, poems, raps, and charts is a delightful way to engage children in the sounds of language and to lay a strong foundation for phonemic awareness. As part of everyday reading of shared text, teachers will implicitly draw attention to print by pointing, masking, and discussing. The enlarged print supports the development of skills in context particularly well; children can focus on features of the text in the totality of a genuine reading experience. The first places where children are apt to join in the reading are those where the layout or the font draws their attention to the words and various aspects of print. The books used in shared reading are designed to enable the teacher to give explicit attention to words, parts of words, letter clusters, and individual letters as the opportunity arises in the authentic reading experience. Emergent readers will initially notice letters and their features, distinguish between letters and words, and focus on words that begin with the same letter as their name, either their first initial or other letters in their name. Early readers will tend to notice letter clusters, word parts that will enable them to problem-solve using analogy, prefixes, and affixes.

My approach to explicit phonics instruction is congruent with Margaret Moustafa's research, which shows that teaching phonics from whole to part allows readers to capitalize on what they already know; in other words, they are taught letter-sound correspondences in words they already know. In Moustafa's words, "Shared reading is an important part of whole to parts phonic instruction. It both demonstrates the reading process to children and establishes a basis for the phonics lessons to come, making the phonics lessons more memorable and, hence, more effective" (1999, p. 451). This view is supported by many researchers, including Marie Clay (1991), who states, "The reader/writer can most easily become articulate about phonological aspects of reading when he is already making use of them—once he is reading and writing small stretches of text" (p. 322).

Shared reading supports the learning of phonics in many ways. Because the books used in shared reading are constructed specifically to support reading and writing development, their layout is designed to capitalize on opportunities for explicit and implicit graphophonic work once the children are familiar with their content and structure.

To model how to use the graphophonic information system, for example, the teacher could cover a few words on a double-page spread (see Figure 3.1; the book used is *Crunchy Munchy*, Parkes 1997).

Figure 3.1

Pig and Goat tried to crawl under the ▢

Cow and Horse tried to ▢ over the fence. But none of them could ▢ the apples.

Pig and Goat tried to crawl under the ☐.

Cow and Horse tried to ☐ over the fence.

But none of them could ☐ the apples.

As the class reads the book, the teacher invites the children to predict each covered word. She responds to their predictions by asking, "What letter would you expect to see at the beginning of that word?" Next she uncovers the initial letter; then she asks, "What letter would you expect to see at the end of that word?" She carefully says the word, then invites the children to confirm or self-correct their prediction before uncovering the whole word, at which point the children can check the visual information.

Recognizing High-Frequency Words

The ability to automatically recognize many high-frequency words allows the reader to maintain a focus on meaning. Shared reading gives children exposure to high-frequency words, which helps them learn to consistently recognize and read them. After they have read a book, children's returning to individual pages to identify and highlight known words in context reinforces recognition. Later, these words can be transferred to the classroom word wall to be used as a resource for writing.

Gay Su Pinnell and Irene Fountas (1998) have identified several broad strategies that readers and writers use to figure out words. Shared reading supports the use of these strategies for problem solving in particular, how words look, and how words connect.

How Words Look

As their store of instantly recognized high-frequency words grows, children can focus their attention on how words look by identifying the clusters and patterns of letters that make up words. Rhymes, poems, and songs such as "Hands, Hands, Hands" (Vaughan 1995) are an excellent starting point for explicit exploration of these features.

Hands can plant. Hands can pick.
Hands can sometimes do a trick.

Hands can tug. Hands can hug.
Hands can hold a wiggly bug.

The first three words of the rhyme are a rich source of information for children to identify the pattern *an*. Wikki Stix™ or highlighter tape can be used to mark the *an* pattern in each of the three words. This provides a clear model as children search the rest of the rhyme, identifying and marking the pattern each time it occurs. As children explore the rhyme to find other recurring patterns, different colors can be used to mark the *ick* and *ug* patterns.

This can be extended to provide experience with onsets and rimes. Onsets are the consonants preceding a vowel in a syllable; rimes are the vowel and any consonant that comes after it. The word *hand* consists of the onset /h/ and the rime /and/.

Collaboratively developed by the teacher and the children, word lists built by combining onsets and rimes are a valuable addition to word walls, both for reading and as a resource for writing. Magnetic letters provide further collaborative and individual exploration allowing children to build and take apart words with patterns.

How Words Connect

Research (Goswami and Bryant 1990) indicates that readers are more able to engage effectively in problem solving when they can use the largest chunks of information available to them. The use of analogy, the ability to recognize and analyze connections in words, allows children to use familiar words to learn unknown words. For example, a reader trying to solve an unfamiliar word such as *canter* might know the first part of the word is *can* and the last part of the word ends like the known word *after*.

Through access to repeated experiences with continuous text, shared reading provides children with the opportunity to work with words and parts of words in secure, meaningful contexts. Familiar texts provide vital support: in order to use analogy, children must be able to recognize a large number of words in context. This provides both contextual and linguistic support. In Moustafa's words, "such an approach underscores the fact that reading is a meaningful activity" (1997, p. 56).

Analogy, then, is best demonstrated through shared reading, to support children's natural ability, as shown in Goswami's research (1990), to make use of this as a problem-solving strategy.

Onsets and rimes provide consistent visual patterns that children can use to problem-solve as well. These are found throughout shared books, in meaningful contexts.

Cloze

As a teaching procedure, cloze is an ideal vehicle to model how readers use the three sources of information in language and to engage children in active problem solving and self-monitoring. Cloze is used by leaving gaps in the flow of oral or written language and inviting children to fill the gaps with words that maintain meaning. Because they are working with continuous text that provides many sources of information, the children have every opportunity to be successful. Cloze can be used to support children in their efforts to predict, check, and confirm a word or to self-correct based on meaning, syntax, and visual information. It can also be used when they are asked to supply another word that means the same thing and to check the suitability of that word from multiple sources of information. Meaning, syntactic patterning, alternative word choices, spelling, and self-monitoring can all be tested and teased out through lively discussion and debate.

Oral Cloze

Children are initially introduced to oral cloze during oral reading of highly predictable texts. The teacher pauses momentarily while reading or falls silent, leaving the children to fill in the gaps, as shown in this example, where the teacher and children are reading *It Didn't Frighten Me* (Goss and Harste 1995).

Teacher: "One pitch black, very dark night, right after dad turned out the—"
Children: Light.
Teacher: "I looked out my window, only to see, an orange alligator up in my—"
Children: Tree.

Teacher: "But that orange—"
Children: Alligator.
Teacher: "Didn't frighten—"
Children: Me!!!

Written Cloze

After many experiences with oral cloze, the teacher introduces the children to written cloze, concealing highly predictable words in the text and having the children use problem-solving strategies to predict the words and then check and confirm their choices. Through many experiences with written cloze children will be able to supply rhyming words and words that sound right and make sense in the flow of the story. In addition, they will be able to justify their choices. Post-it notes, which come in various sizes, are an ideal material to use in covering the words in this activity.

Words selected for cloze are not chosen randomly. The teacher bases the decision of what words should be covered on the particular problem-solving strategies he or she wishes to discuss and on an awareness of just how children can use the text in concert with their background knowledge and experience. During the activity, the teacher guides and challenges the children to use multiple sources of information to survey, predict, check, confirm, and self-correct.

In the following example the teacher has chosen to use a nonfiction text, *A Closer Look* (Lunis 1999). The children read the whole text together, pausing briefly at each missing word and letting their minds supply a meaningful word. Pausing and thinking, rather than having the teacher fill in the space by saying "blank," allows children to maintain their flow of meaningful thought. This emulates how oral cloze was modeled.

A Closer Look

You can use tools to observe things that are far away.

Binoculars make faraway things ☐ closer. Scientists use binoculars to observe animals in ☐ natural habitats.

Make your own ☐ . In each photograph, name details that binoculars could ☐ you see.

Teacher: As you read this the first time, join in if you can, or just listen. I'll pause briefly at the missing words to let you predict them in your minds. (*He reads the passage, then asks about the concealed words.*) What would make sense in the first gap?

Riana: *Seem.*

Teacher: Yes. *Seem* would fit in there. Do any other words make sense there?

Bess: *Look* makes sense. Binoculars make things look closer.

Teacher: Let's have a look at the first letter. (*He peels the cover back to show the* L.)

Children: *Looks.*

Teacher (*uncovering the whole word*): The author has used *look*. What did you decide for the next gap?

Jeri: *Their.* He's talking about the animals' habitats.

Teacher: I like the way you are thinking. Let's read what we have so far.

Jeri: *Observations* goes in the next gap.

Teacher: It could. Tell us about your thinking, Jeri.

Jeri: When we read "scientists use binoculars to observe" again I just changed *observe* into *observations.*

Teacher: Nice work. Sometimes it helps to read something again. It's a helpful strategy. Now what do you all think the last word is going to be?

All: *Help*!!!

Teacher: Let's look and see...

In short, the supportive context of shared reading provides a meaningful way for the teacher to:

- show genuine enjoyment in reading
- model how readers think and act
- model fluent, phrased reading
- build on the interests and abilities of the learners
- teach book and print conventions
- continually extend invitations for learners to increase their active participation
- ensure the use of various skills and strategies for reading and comprehending
- explore semantics, syntax, and graphophonics
- engage children in talk about texts
- demonstrate the relationship between reading and writing
- show how to read for different purposes
- balance implicit and explicit teaching

4

Shared Reading in Action

The style of teaching . . . might be called invitational—an enthusiastic invitation to participate, contribute, take over the operation.

Don Holdaway

In the classrooms I work in, a shared book session typically runs for 30 to 40 minutes each day. Each session has the following elements:

- It begins with the rereading of a favorite resource or resources chosen by the children. Selections may include songs, poems, and chants as well as big books. During this time the focus is on enjoyment and fluent, phrased reading. The reading is followed by a brief exploration of some point in the language or illustrations the children have decided to focus on.
- The session continues with either the introduction of a new resource or the revisiting of another resource for in-depth rereading and discussion.
- The session ends with an explicit mini-lesson. This is based on ongoing assessment and is used to demonstrate a skill, strategy, or behavior the teacher wants to introduce or reinforce. The mini-lesson focuses attention on some aspect of language in continuous text, using a known book. Sometimes the mini-lesson is unplanned, and has come about as a result of the children's particular interest in some feature of a book being shared. These teachable moments are golden, and it's always a good idea to act

on students' needs and interests. The lesson that was planned will keep until the next day.

Guided reading immediately follows shared reading. Organizing the program this way lets the teacher draw on shared reading experiences for independent small-group work that is meaningful and relevant and that provides the children with further practice applying the skills and strategies. It also helps solve the perennial question of what to do with the others during guided reading.

Rereading Favorite Resources

On a typical day in Ms. Goodwin's grade 1 classroom the whole group is informally gathered together on a carpeted area of the room. There is an air of expectancy as they wait to begin. Ms. Goodwin is seated on a low chair beside an easel, with a collection of materials for sharing within easy reach. These resources include a pointer; commercially produced big books representing a range of authors, illustrators, and genres; poem, song, and rhyme posters; some materials written collaboratively by the teacher and children; and blank paper.

Although the grouping appears relaxed, all children are seated in a way that gives each an unobstructed view of the book displayed on the easel. All can see the pictures and print, and all are expected to participate in the shared reading at their current level of understanding.

Ms. Goodwin begins the session by inviting the children to choose the resource they would like to read first. She then invites one child to point to the print and one to turn the pages. The current favorite is read exuberantly.

The focus is on enjoyment and maintaining meaning over continuous text. The children participate confidently and enthusiastically. Ms. Goodwin uses this time to closely observe several of the children's interactions with the text. She will use this information to plan which books she will later use and how she will use them in subsequent shared reading sessions.

Why Rereading Favorites Is Important

The practice of rereading favorite books has been extensively researched in both home and school settings (Sulzby 1985; Yaden 1988; Parkes

1990a). One of the major findings was that repeated readings of children's favorite texts, either independently or with an experienced reader, consistently resulted in new explorations and learning. As the children revisited texts over an extended period of time, each successful experience built confidence and led to their increased participation and exploration. The children took responsibility for more and more of the reading until finally they were able to read the books largely independently. Ms. Goodwin capitalizes on this research by inviting children to choose the books for reading and rereading. She also makes sure that the children have time and access to the shared books for small-group and independent rereading.

By revisiting old favorites and exploring new texts together, the children in Ms. Goodwin's classroom:

- develop and refine a network of strategies for predicting, checking, confirming, and self-correcting
- experience a sense of community and personal achievement as they grow as readers through these social experiences
- build a solid, secure base of known books, which acts as a springboard for exploring the new

Ways to Vary the Rereading

Ms. Goodwin uses every opportunity to model and engage the children in the use of various cueing systems. This systematic attention to making explicit the ways all aspects of language support one another lays the foundation for self-monitoring and self-correcting behavior as the children develop as readers and writers. As the children enjoy their chosen texts each day, the teacher supports reading and meaning by constantly varying the purposes of her invitations for them to actively participate. During one reading, for example, they might be invited to clap the rhythm of a repetitive chant such as:

Run, run,
As fast as you can.
You can't catch me.
I'm the Gingerbread Man!

This sets a purpose for children to focus on visual information, as they look for the written language that signals when to begin clapping and reading. In addition, their clapping to the rhythm of the language emphasizes the syntactic pattern of the text. Knowledge of how language should flow to sound right is a powerful tool for self-correction.

On another day she might encourage them to form groups to read the dialogue of different characters in unison. This time the purpose is not only to have the children monitor the print closely and recognize when to join in, but also to use suitable pitch intonation and stress to bring the characters to life.

On yet another occasion she will use oral cloze to encourage children to actively monitor meaning and to use the cue systems in an integrated way to predict and confirm.

Ms. Goodwin (*pointing and reading*): "Come, said the crocodile, Come to tea, And he ate up the zebra One, two, —"
Children: *Three!!*
Ms. Goodwin: What helped you know that?
Charlie: *Three* rhymes with *tea*.
Amelia: And it comes next: one, two, *three*.
Meridith: *Three* begins with *th* like *the*.
Ms. Goodwin: I like the way you worked that out. You used a rhyming clue and a meaning clue and checked that the beginning letters matched your prediction.
Charlie: Let's do another one…

Deepening Student Involvement

When the children are able to read familiar texts with confidence and success they can pay closer attention to particular features of the text and expand their knowledge about how print works and how print and pictures work together. They know Ms. Goodwin expects them to be active problem solvers, and they love the challenge of finding new things to share.

After reading the favorite each day, the teacher asks an open-ended question, such as "What was one new thing you noticed about the book today?" The following example shows how this unfolds in the classroom. In this example the children have just chosen to read *Goodnight, Goodnight* (Parkes 1989).

Ms. Goodwin: What was one new thing you noticed about the book today?

Figure 4.1

Bernard: I saw a shadow in the pictures on pages 12 and 13. [See Figure 4.1.]

Ms. Goodwin: Let's turn to that page and look together. Show us what you saw, Bernard.

Bernard (*tracing around the outline with his finger*): See? There it is! It's an alligator.

Milo: Yeah. I see it too. It's not an alligator. It's the fox!

Ms. Goodwin: What makes you think that?

Milo: I can see the shape. And the fox is in that story. The fox tricked the gingerbread boy and ate him.

Ms. Goodwin: So you think the fox is waiting for him when he jumps through the window?

Bernard: Yeah. That's what I think too.

Ms. Goodwin: So the author and illustrator put it there as a clue to help our thinking. I wonder if they gave us any more shadow clues. Let's have a look. (*She turns to pages 6 and 7.*)

Carl: The bears! I can see bear shapes!

Ms. Goodwin: Show me where. Oh yes, I can see them now. What do they help you to know?

Carl: That it's Goldilocks. You know! *Goldilocks and the Three Bears.*

Bernard: Let's look and find some more shadow clues.

Ms. Goodwin: I'll leave the book on the easel later so your group can look some more during guided reading.

Each time a child shares what he or she has noticed serves as a model for other children. While the example above focused on looking for details in picture clues and making inferences based on these clues, the next example focuses on phonological and graphological information.

The children have chosen *Goodnight, Goodnight* again. Paul has noticed that a number of words end with *ing*.

Paul: I saw there were lots of words that end with ing.

Ms. Goodwin: Show us where.

Bernard: There's one on the Mother Hubbard page. See?

Paul (*quoting from the book*): "Who's that *looking*?"

Ms. Goodwin: Let's put highlighter tape over the *ing* in *looking*.

Paul: The Goldilocks part has another one. (*He finds* climbing *and carefully highlights it.*)

Ms. Goodwin: Are there any more?

Paul: Yes. I saw one on the gingerbread page.

Ms. Goodwin: Turn to the page, please, Bernard, and see if everyone can find it…

They continue locating and highlighting *ing* words in the book. The teacher concludes the lesson by writing *climbing, looking*, and *running*. Then she explains how the consonant is doubled when adding *ing* to *running* and tells the children they will be able to use that strategy for themselves when they are writing.

On another occasion, after the children reread a favorite book the teacher might ask, "What did you choose to work on especially today?" This lets the children know that they should set themselves purposes for reading and be on the lookout for new connections and understandings as they reread the books.

In the following example a group of kindergarteners in Mr. Fawcett's class have chosen *The Little Red Hen* (Parkes 1985).

Mr. Fawcett: What did you work on today?

Peta: I read all the "Not I"s when you pointed to them.

Mr. Fawcett: I noticed how well you did that. It was a good part of the book to work on. Will you please show us how you recognized them?

Peta: They are all in a line down the page and they're all the same. And they all have those things (*points to the speech marks*) around them.

Gino: I tried to remember the noises the animals made so I knew who was talking.

Mr. Fawcett: What do you mean, Gino?

Gino: You know. When it says "Not I, barked." I knew it would be the dog because dogs bark.

Mr. Fawcett: I like the way you figured that out. Let's show everyone your strategy.

They locate one of the repetitive refrains, and Mr. Fawcett uses oral cloze to invite Gino to read with him and demonstrate his strategy to the rest of the class.

Mr. Fawcett (*reading*): "Not I, barked—"

Gino: the dog.

Mr. Fawcett: "Not I, grunted—"

Gino: the pig.

Next Mr. Fawcett says, "Let's put highlighter tape over the words that describe each animal's sound to help us all remember to use your strategy." He then highlights

"Not I," **barked** the dog.

"Not I," **meowed** the cat.

"Not I," **grunted** the pig.

"Not I," **quacked** the duck.

The following day, the children again choose *The Little Red Hen* as the favorite. Before they read, Mr. Fawcett reminds them of Gino's contribution on the previous day. As they read together he capitalizes on the previous day's work by initially emphasizing *barked, meowed*, and so on. Then he stops in mid-sentence to let the children complete each sentence.

These examples closely replicate the spirit and content of the bedtime story, where an experienced reader responds to a child's lead, deepening and enriching the experience.

Asking what new things they have noticed after the children have enjoyed their favorite story encourages them not only to enjoy reading but also to actively monitor the meaning of the words, attend closely to pictures and print, and set their own purposes for reading. It also provides children with authentic reasons to talk about their thinking, their growing insights about books and reading, and their use of skills and strategies. Such activities combine to provide powerful models and learning opportunities for all members of the group as well as assessment and teaching opportunities for the teacher.

Revisiting a Recently Introduced Resource

Ms. Goodwin's class was introduced to the book *When Goldilocks Went to the House of the Bears* (Greene, Pollock, and Scarfe 1995) the previous week. Their knowledge of the story line and the catchy song are both strong supports, and many of them are able to join in, reading a large amount of the text. Today Ms. Goodwin is working to increase participation in the reading. She suggests that the large group divide into two groups, with each responsible for reading a part. Because she has two ESL learners in the group, she invites all the children to mime the actions as they read. This adds another layer of meaning to help the ESL children comprehend the text.

Before the two-part reading, Ms. Goodwin skims through the book and, with the children's help, quickly identifies and highlights the text for each group by placing alternating strips of red and green highlighter tape down the margin to show where to read.

In this brief revisiting, Ms. Goodwin has provided:

- a retelling and a survey of the illustrations as she discussed where to place the highlighter tape in the book
- an opportunity for more experienced members of the group to maintain meaning over continuous text
- support for less experienced readers to increase their participation

Introducing a New Book

Effective introductions of new books vary depending on the book, the group of children, and the purpose for using it.

The introduction can begin with the teacher reading the title and author and building background through discussion about the title and the cover pictures. If the children have already read books by that author, it is useful to recall the kinds of books that author writes as part of their background experience and their anticipation of the content. Alternatively, the introduction can begin with the teacher asking the children to predict the title and content from the cover picture and then guiding discussion about it.

It is *not* necessary, however, and is even counterproductive, to do a picture or book walk before reading the book with the children. While looking through the entire book as preparation for reading it is a perfectly valid part of guided reading with emergent readers, it is not part of shared reading, as it takes away the excitement as well as most of the children's work! A discussion about the cover information and perhaps the first couple of pages is usually plenty to introduce the book, make connections between the book and the prior knowledge and experience of the children, and have them begin their thinking about the book.

I have found that much of the craft of writing books for shared reading lies in providing opportunities for the children to unfold the story gradually, page by page, and for rich, ongoing discussion as they do so. Only by doing the work themselves can children develop a network of strategies for thinking and acting like readers and become self-motivated, self-regulated learners.

In some classrooms, during the first reading the children focus mainly on listening and watching as the teacher points to the text and reads. However, they are always invited to join in the reading wherever they can. At several points, the teacher wonders aloud what might happen next, or falls silent at a highly predictable word. The invitation to actively participate is done quickly so as to focus the children's thinking and attention and to give them initial entry points into the book without spoiling the flow of the meaning or language.

In other classrooms, teachers make the first reading very conversational and interactive, almost a browsing discussion through the book. This is how I prefer to introduce many big books. Although I always know the book well, and in many instances have already shared it with other groups of children, I don't have a prepared set of prompts and questions or a set way of reading the book. Instead, I try to create an atmosphere that invites the children to interact with any aspect of the book as active collaborators with me and that sets up a lively paced, ongoing dialogue throughout the session.

The children's thoughts and their strategies for predicting, checking, and making inferences provide rich models for the children to learn from each other, and give me a clear view of their thought processes. This way of introducing new texts can be used very effectively in groups where there are many ESL students. The teachers are able to build bridges between the language and concepts of the children and those of the book by developing a rich learning environment that fosters dialogue, understanding, and language acquisition.

Informational texts are introduced differently from narrative texts, mainly because an informational book is usually read by "dipping in" and focusing on a single section rather than reading it from cover to cover. Informational texts are discussed more fully in Chapter 7.

A Kindergarten Introduction to a Well-Known Tale

Let's take a look at how one kindergarten teacher introduces a new book to his class. Because he knows that many of the children are familiar with other versions of the story of *The Gingerbread Man* (Parkes 1986), Mr. Malcolm introduces the book by showing the cover and inviting the children to tell what they know about the story.

Mr. Malcolm: Some of you may have heard this story before.
Mario: I know that story. It's the Gingerbread Man.
Jessie: Me too. He runs away. And he says, "Run, run, as fast as you can—"
Several children (*taking up the refrain*): "You can't catch me. I'm the Gingerbread Man!"
Maria: I've got a gingerbread book like that.
Marco: Lots of people chase him.
Connie: They want to eat him.
Mr. Malcolm: Can you remember who chases him?
Jessie: A man and a woman.
Mario: And a cat and a dog.

Aaron: The wolf eats him.

Mario: No. It's a fox. He goes *snip, snap* and eats him.

Mr. Malcolm: You know a lot about the story. Watch and listen as I read it for the first time and join in wherever you can. What words will we see and hear first?

Children: "Once upon a time . . ."

Mr. Malcolm: You're right! Once upon a time . . .

Mr. Malcolm reads the story with obvious enjoyment, using facial expressions and gestures. He skillfully uses oral cloze to invite participation, pausing briefly to invite or confirm children's predictions. He keeps the focus on meaning by sometimes thinking out loud, "I wonder what will happen next?" and models book conventions by adding, "Let's turn the page and see." A discussion about personal responses to the text follows the reading.

Mr. Malcolm: I loved the way you all joined in. Which is your favorite part of the story?

Jake: When the Gingerbread Man jumps out of the oven!

Mr. Malcolm: Let's have a look at that page again. How do you think the old man and woman feel?

Aaron: Mad.

Mr. Malcolm: What makes you think that, Aaron?

Aaron: Look at the old man's mouth. He's yelling at him.

Connie: I think they're mad at him because they can't eat him!

Mr. Malcolm elicits one or two more responses to get the children personally involved. As the children give their comments he encourages them to look for detail in the illustrations that support their ideas.

At the children's request, he reads the book again, inviting them to join in wherever they can. To encourage this behavior he stops reading from time to time, using oral cloze to let the children take over highly predictable parts of the text. He emphasizes rhyme and rhythm by inviting them to supply a rhyming word as he reads

Run, run,
As fast as you can.
You can't catch me.
I'm the Gingerbread _____!

He concludes by suggesting that they might read it again the next day.

Returning to the Text

Over the next few days the class returns to the book for rereading and discussion. Mr. Malcolm encourages the children to take over more and more of the reading. Some days they use percussion instruments to emphasize the rhythm; other days they click their fingers or clap their hands. A great deal of implicit teaching takes place during these revisitings. Mr. Malcolm encourages the children to notice details as they talk about the print and pictures and constantly reinforces book and print concepts as he talks and models.

Before long, the children have taken complete responsibility for reading the repetitive refrain. Observing this, he prepares to increase their involvement by shifting responsibility to them for another part of the story.

Mr. Malcolm: Who can remember how the story begins?
Children: "Once upon a time . . ."
Mr. Malcolm: Show me how you read it. I'll do the pointing.

When the children are able to join in to read much of the text, he varies their involvement. He has them:

- take responsibility for reading particular character parts
- vary the ways they read the refrain
- dramatize the story
- mime the actions
- take turns pointing to the text while the others read

Each rereading strengthens the children's understanding of the meaning of the story and the structure of the language. This provides a solid foundation for later work with specific visual features of the text.

Focusing on Visual Features of Text

Some weeks later, after the book has become well known to the children, Mr. Malcolm uses it to engage them in explicit word analysis, focusing on onset and rime. This includes showing how to analyze both letters and letter clusters and patterns. Research (Goswami and Bryant 1990; Adams 1995) has shown that children are able to use the visual patterns contained in rimes, combined with onsets, to figure out words.

Onsets are the opening part of the word; the rime, which contains the vowel, completes the word. Although rime is different from rhyme, if two words such as *can* and *man* have the same rime, or word ending (*an*), they may also rhyme. Because children need to be able to hear the rime before working with it in its written form, Mr. Malcolm chooses two known words that do rhyme.

He knows they have previously listened and played with the rhyming patterns in the refrain and are able to identify them in oral language. Today he uses this prior knowledge to have the children focus on identifying patterns in written language using the words *can* and *man*.

Mr. Malcolm: There are two words that rhyme in this part of the story. Listen and watch the words as I point and read them to you. See if you can tell me which ones they are.

Pointing to each word in turn, he reads, putting a slight emphasis on the rhyming words:

> Run, run,
> As fast as you *can*.
> You can't catch me.
> I'm the Gingerbread *Man*!

Alonzo: I can hear them. *Can* and *man*.
Mr. Malcolm: Can you show me the word *man*, Alonzo?
Alonzo (*pointing*): There it is! And there's *can*!
Mr. Malcolm: Nice job. Let's put some highlighter tape over those words. Now I want you all to look closely at the words *can* and *man*. What do you notice about them?
Connie: I can see the same letters in them.
Mr. Malcolm: Where?
Connie (*pointing*): At the end. See? They both end with *an*.
Mr. Malcolm: Yes. The words both have the same pattern.
Alonzo: But they have a different letter at the beginning. (*He frames the word parts.*)
Mr. Malcolm: The first letter helps you to check if the word is *can* or

man. (He writes can *and* man *on a white board using a different color to identify the word parts.)*

Next he writes two more *an*'s and invites the children to think of beginning letters to make new words. He encourages them to use the alphabet to find beginning letters that might work in combination with the rime *an*.

To further reinforce the concept he has the children make the two words on a magnetic board, using different colors for the onset and the rime. He then lines up a row of *an*'s immediately below the children's two words and challenges them to add onsets to build more words.

During the year, *The Gingerbread Man* will be revisited for other explicit teaching as the need arises.

Mr. Malcolm might also use the book to model and engage children in writing. The children could:

- participate in written cloze, focusing on semantic, syntactic, and graphophonic cue systems
- alter the text at the word, phrase, and sentence level
- change characters, settings, or events

Because of the memorable language, which makes it easy to read, the potential for mime and drama, and the different character parts, *The Gingerbread Man* is sure to be picked on other occasions as the children's chosen favorite.

Skill and Strategy Teaching

I always use well-known books as the basis for explicit instruction. Because children have read and reread these books, they are familiar with both the content and the structure and can therefore give their full attention to the strategy being taught. Their familiarity with content and structure provides them with a framework that allows them to use multiple sources of information. For example, if they are asked to replace a word with another word with the same meaning, they can read the surrounding text to check and confirm that their choice is meaningful in that context and that it fits the structure of the language.

The word *explicit* does not mean the book will be used to skill, drill, and ultimately kill the learners' interest and enthusiasm for the book.

The teaching is done in a conversational way in the context of the whole text. The children are invited to engage in problem solving by thinking like authors and illustrators and considering why particular language and illustrative choices have been made.

In the following example, Ms. Goodwin uses the text *Goodnight, Goodnight* for implicit instruction. Today the purpose of the lesson is to model how to integrate multiple sources of information to solve problems and to engage children in doing so. *Goodnight, Goodnight* was designed for this purpose. It provides many opportunities for children to use prior knowledge through picture clues, language clues, print clues, and intertextual clues.

Focusing the children's attention on the cover of the book, Ms. Goodwin briefly models how to look for clues that support meaning in the title and cover illustration.

Ms. Goodwin: Today we are going to search for clues the author and illustrator provided to help us read this book. (*She points to the title.*) Think about the words *Goodnight, Goodnight.* What clues do they give you about the story?

Ramona: That it happens at night.

Marcia: The words are blue, and look (*pointing*), there's little stars inside the words.

Sue: That it's a fun story about a good night.

Ms. Goodwin (*opening the book to display the entire cover*): What clues do the illustrations give you?

Sue: They all look like they're having fun.

James: She's reading to them. You could think she is baby-sitting and wants them to go to sleep.

Ramona: They all look weird!

Jennifer: The pictures tell you who the characters are in the story. The beanstalk and the hen help you to know it's Jack.

Sue (*excitedly*): And look! The dog is a clue for Mother Hubbard.

As the children search for clues and identify the characters from familiar nursery rhymes and traditional tales, the teacher builds a framework for them to use intertextual clues by asking them to recall some of the things the characters say and do in their stories.

Next the children read the first two pages (Figure 4.2):

I love to read
in bed at night.
Then Teddy and I
turn out the light.

And as we dream
the night away,
our storybook friends
come out to play.

Who's that looking
in my cupboard?
It's my friend, Old ...

2

3

Figure 4.2

Who's that looking
in my cupboard?
It's my friend, Old…

As the children predict "Mother Hubbard," Ms. Goodwin challenges
them to justify their answer. Through discussion and attention to detail
in the print and illustration they identify the rhyming clue of *cupboard*
and *Hubbard*, the picture clue of the woman looking in the cupboard
with her dog at her feet, the Mother Goose poster on the bedroom wall,
and the word clue of the first word of the character's name.

Ms. Goodwin challenges the children to use letter-sound knowledge
to think about what letter each word in the name *Mother Hubbard* will
begin and end with. They then turn the page and use visual information
to read and confirm their prediction. One child, who has insisted that
the name will be Mother Goose, self-corrects. Together they chant the
rhyming text on those two pages (Figure 4.3).

Figure 4.3

They then move on to the next two-page spread (Figure 4.4). The children predict that the character is Goldilocks and check the print to confirm their prediction. All are sure that the following page will show the Three Bears because "they go with Goldilocks." One child notices shadowy shapes of the three bears and excitedly shows this clue to the others. Ms. Goodwin asks the children for ways they can check their predictions about the Three Bears. Replies include

- "There will be three words."
- "We can check the pictures."
- "We can check the first letters."

Ms. Goodwin asks what letters the children expect to see before turning the page to confirm their prediction.

Together the children and teacher continue to read and think their way through the text predicting, checking, and confirming by using the

Figure 4.4

multiple clues in the written language and the illustrations. Some pages include verbatim language clues from the featured characters' stories to increase the challenge and to provide situations where self-correction is likely to occur.

Ms. Goodwin draws the lesson to a close by having the children nominate one other well-known storybook character that could have been included in *Goodnight, Goodnight*. They recall characters from books they know, thinking about the picture and language clues they could provide for readers to figure out who their character was. Together they write a list of the clues.

Language clue	**Illustration clue**
Who's that walking through the wood?	flowers a red cloak
Who has to leave the ball at 12?	coach glass slipper
Who was frightened from her tuffet?	spider bowl and spoon

Later in the day, this activity forms the basis for a shared writing lesson, where the children write and illustrate an episode for their chosen character based on the structure of *Goodnight, Goodnight*. For example, the two-page spread would read "Who's that running through the wood?/ It's Little Red . . ." with the following page completing the name: "Riding Hood."

The children's completed pages are displayed as models. During center time over the next two weeks the children write and illustrate more pages based on other characters. These innovations will form the basis for a new shared book.

In this typical shared book session, the teacher has:

- enabled all the children in the class to take part in reading and writing
- demonstrated how books work and how readers read
- involved the children in thinking, talking, listening, viewing, and reading
- provided implicit and explicit instruction in skill and strategy use
- involved the children in predicting, searching, checking, confirming, and self-correcting using multiple sources of information, including meaning, structure and visual cues, prior knowledge, and text-to-text connections
- engaged the children in writing that took them beyond the book
- involved the children in problem solving on continuous text

Using Shared Books for Independent and Small-Group Work

Following the large-group session Ms. Goodwin gathers a small group together for guided reading. During small-group work it is important that the rest of the children be able to work independently. Independent activities can stem from the work the children have done with shared books. Purposeful, meaningful activities based on shared reading can help children consolidate and extend their learning.

A look at what is going on in Ms. Goodwin's classroom provides examples of possible small-group and independent activities.

Listen and Read

A group of four is working with an audio recording of a shared book. Each child has a copy of the book and reads along with the recording. The recording presents the story in several ways. In the first version, the reader uses dramatic voices in rendering the story. The children may choose just to listen, or to listen and read along. The second version is accompanied by music. Again, the children can either listen or join in the reading. The third version is oral cloze, with expressive music filling the gaps and helping to support meaning and cue the children in their responses. Made by professional actors and musicians, these recordings provide scaffolds, helping children to build toward independence with the books and enjoy reading. Using the various readings on the recordings, the children practice reading the book more than once, yet the experiences are engaging enough to keep their interest. This type of activity provides excellent support for ESL learners.

Read It Again

Three children are gathered at the easel with a collection of familiar big books. Each has a pointer that they use to follow the print as they reread self-selected texts together (see the photograph on the next page). With this smaller group, each child must contribute, and together they have enough knowledge and experience to problem-solve and read their way through the books they choose. Self-monitoring and self-correcting of book and print concepts and meaning and structure are reinforced in the context of a meaningful experience.

At the opposite end of the classroom a pair of children are rereading songs and rhymes using the overhead projector and transparencies. The pair take turns pointing to the words with a thin piece of dowel as they read and sing in unison.

Two children work together to read a big book. One child has chosen to reread part of the page while the other checks out what they will read on the next page.

Word Matching

Two groups of three children each have a big book and several high-frequency words written on Post-it notes. Each child in the group chooses a word, then skim-reads the book to find and match their word. When all the words have been found, the group reads their book together, emphasizing the matching words.

Onsets and Rimes

The shared book *The Three Little Pigs* (Parkes and Smith 1986) is propped up at the table. Ms. Goodwin has used Wikki Stix™ to identify the high-frequency word *pig*, which can be broken into onset and rime. Together, she and the children brainstormed a list of *ig* words during shared reading, as shown in the photograph on the next page.

The children wrote a list of words by adding onsets to the rime ig.

Working with plastic letters, two children first use the words from the book as a model to construct the highlighted words. Following this, they each build new words by combining new onsets with the basic rime (see the photograph on the next page). They compare lists and read them to each other.

Ms. Goodwin taped some magnetic letters together to make other rimes, such as *ame, ack, ell, ice,* and *ot.* When the children have shared their original list they choose another rime and work in pairs to select onsets and make new words.

Community Cloze

A number of words in a shared text have been covered with blank paper. A group of four has been provided with a set of word cards and must choose those that will meaningfully fill the blanks. This activity involves a good deal of prediction, checking, self-correcting, and discussion. When the children have completed the task, they read the text together.

When Goldilocks went to the house of the ▯ .   counted

Oh what did her blue ▯ see?   eyes

The children read the new words they made by combining new onsets with the rime.

A bear that was ⬚ . | bears |

A ⬚ that was small. | that |

A bear ⬚ was tiny and that was all. | large |

She ⬚ them 1, 2, 3. | bear |

Independent Reading

Multiple copies of the small-book versions of the big book are readily accessible for independent reading. The children in another group of four choose to read either silently or with a buddy. Each child has a five-minute tape, and the group has access to a tape recorder. Children can record themselves reading a self-selected book and then play the tape back. This practice reading continuous text helps build speed and accuracy, which in turn supports fluency and phrasing.

Build a Story

Another small group is sequencing sentence strips on a pocket chart. The strips are turned facedown to begin with, and each child selects one

The children read the first sentence strip and check to see that it matches the picture.

or two. The child who has the first line of the text reads it to the group and tells why he or she thinks it is first. Each child reads a selected strip and justifies its position. When the text is complete, the group reads it together (see the photograph above).

These and related small-group activities provide children with a range of authentic purposes for returning to a book and deepening their understanding of its content as well as the reading/writing process generally.

5

How Shared Reading Contributes to the Other Components of a Balanced Literacy Program

A balanced reading program includes a range of literacy activities, carefully selected materials for each activity, and a responsive teacher.

Linda J. Dorn, Cathy French, and Tammy Jones

Shared reading is the driving force underlying a balanced literacy program and contributes to all aspects of it. The texts used in shared reading should always initially be above the current reading level of the learners, thereby immersing and engaging them in new experiences, new language and language structures, and new topics and concepts. This ensures the teacher is able to work at the frontier of development where more challenging tasks are conducive to learning. As the books become familiar and the children take increasing control of strategies for reading and comprehending them, they provide the basis for small-group and independent work. This makes the children both return to the resources and go beyond them in a recursive cycle of reading, revisiting, rereading, retelling, reflecting, and reshaping.

Shared Reading and Oral Language Development

Readers' oral language is their primary source for anticipating what may happen next in the text and checking whether their reading makes sense (Clay 1991). Shared reading can be used to reinforce and build on the oral language each child has and supports continued development in a number of ways. The large pictures and photographs provide a context for meaning making and a catalyst for discussion as children are supported to see the connections between their prior knowledge and experiences and those of the book.

Facilitated by a responsive teacher, these conversations weave together the children's life experiences, the meaning potential provided by the author and illustrator, and the children's experiences with other written texts. As the discussion of the text unfolds, the language provides models of vocabulary and syntax while the content of the book supports meaning and concept development. All of this is particularly helpful for ESL learners.

Each time children revisit a shared resource as an interactive experience to think, talk, and read, they use these multiple ways of communicating to take part in a conversation through a text.

As children explore books together, the opportunity to communicate through language in a variety of supportive contexts, and for different purposes, expands their vocabulary and their facility with language. In addition to this, they become familiar with various forms of written language, and they add this knowledge to their growing repertoire of how and why language can be used.

Building on and Extending the Read-Aloud Experience

As cited in Chapter 1, studies show that reading aloud from good children's literature is extremely beneficial for children and provides a solid foundation for helping them learn to read. Being read to by a teacher who knows and loves books helps build community in a classroom through a storehouse of common experiences and provides motivation for learners of all ages to learn to read, and to read. It is an essential component of a balanced literacy program.

At the earliest levels the read-aloud experience immerses children in pleasurable experiences with books carefully chosen for their age and experience and teaches them to love books and reading. Research documenting children's experiences during repeated readings of self-selected favorites (Yaden 1988 and Sulzby 1985) provides compelling evidence to support the rereading of loved books. When these books are reread on request and made available for children to return to and browse through independently, children begin to reconstruct the story from the pictures and their memory of the text using a mixture of written and oral language structures. During repeated experiences they deepen their involvement in many ways as they notice details in illustrations, internalize the rhythm of the language, enter into a dialogue with the books, and relate the content to their own experiences.

Reading aloud continues to delight and challenge children through the grade levels, opening the way to new authors and new ways of sharing information. At the same time, it helps them develop a sense of story, concepts, language, and a knowledge of theme, plot, and characterization; and the books provide models of how writers think and present their ideas.

Shared reading complements and extends the read-aloud experience. It enables children to apply their knowledge about how books work to learning to read for themselves.

Extending the Range of Familiar Books for Independent Reading

While some students enter school with rich, varied experiences with books, others come from homes where being read to plays no part in their daily lives. For these students, shared reading in conjunction with the classroom read-aloud program helps them build a store of familiar books that they have come to enjoy through many classroom readings, rereadings, and discussions. For more experienced students the shared reading sessions provide an opportunity for them to orchestrate their own ways of responding to print.

Providing Writing Models

To become writers, children need to be involved in many experiences where writing is demonstrated in purposeful ways and where they are included as active participants in thinking and decision making. Shared reading from a range of text types provides powerful models for children's own writing. Used effectively to promote "creative interactions" (Cambourne 1998), it encourages children to read like writers as they learn to engage with the authors' thinking and consider why they have made particular choices about purpose, topic, and language. In Figure 5.1, for example, children have replaced the characters and action from *Goodnight, Goodnight* (Parkes 1989) with characters from well-known shared books. This section features Joy Cowley's much loved Meanies.

Because most shared books lend themselves to written innovations at the word, phrase, or whole-text level, they also invite children to write like readers and incorporate some of the ideas, language, and written language structures of the original text. When I write for children and teachers I purposely choose my topic, language, and layout to make the books easy for teachers and children to write innovations. One of my greatest delights in life is to receive copies of these books through the mail with letters from children, telling me about their writing. Some years ago I received a letter from some children who had been reading one of my big books, *Who's in the Shed?* (Parkes 1986). Their letter concluded like this:

> We used some of the ideas and we wrote our own big book.
> We like our book the best.

No words could have made me happier.

The Foundation for Guided Reading

The skills and strategies children are expected to use in guided reading can be taught during shared reading. The books are designed to help teachers model and involve students in the use of problem-solving strategies. These include:

- using background knowledge and experiences
- working with meaning using structural and visual clues
- orchestrating the cueing systems
- recognizing the language features, conventions, and organization of different written texts
- using illustrations, charts, photographs, and diagrams

Figure 5.1

- using multiple sources of information
- predicting, checking, and confirming

Specific examples of how this unfolds in the classroom are included in later chapters.

I see and hear of many instances where children do not have the benefit of shared reading to prepare them for the largely independent reading of guided reading books. Not surprisingly, these children have problems later when they are put into guided reading groups without a solid foundation of skills, strategies, or behaviors or the continued support of shared reading to reinforce these understandings using a variety of materials.

As shown in the accompanying table, shared reading and guided reading are interwoven practices. Students practice using strategies for themselves in small-group guided reading lessons and have these strategies reinforced and extended as the teacher uses increasingly complex texts during shared reading. Careful observation of children working in both these instructional settings provides valuable data to guide the choice and use of appropriate books for shared and guided reading.

Shared Reading	**Guided Reading**
Demonstrates the reading process	Asks children to apply aspects of the reading process with increasing independence
Invites participation in reading and reading behaviors within the security of a large group	Expects participation in independent problem solving within a small group
Builds knowledge about books and print	Has children apply knowledge about books and print
Draws on teacher and group support	Uses some teacher and group support
Implicitly and explicitly demonstrates and invites participation in strategies for reading	Challenges the reader to draw on aspects of demonstration to process novel text
Provides models for use of skills	Has children apply skills
Provides models of and encourages strategic use of phonological and graphological information	Challenges readers to use phonological and graphological information to predict, check, and confirm
Creates a store of familiar texts	Extends the range of texts available for independent reading
Introduces a variety of books and language structures	Has children apply their knowledge to an increasing variety of books and language structures

The Basis for Small-Group Work

Because the texts in shared reading have already been used many times and in many ways they are comfortable resources for children to use independently in small-group work. The familiar texts provide children with reading and writing practice; they also provide support for children to revisit and reflect on them in challenging yet achievable ways (see Chapters 4 and 8 for ideas and activities).

The opportunity to revisit the texts for many different purposes increases children's familiarity with their content and allows them to deepen their understanding of meaning, structure, and visual information as well as form and purpose. This familiarity provides another step on the road to reading independently.

Here are some suggestions for small-group activities using shared reading resources:

- Children may enjoy working in pairs at an easel with the big books and pointers. Initially this allows them to practice reading with increased independence. Later it provides the practice they need to learn how to process text automatically and achieve fluent, phrased reading. This activity is particularly helpful for supporting ESL learners.
- Audiotapes support the reading of the small-book copies or the big books themselves and can also be used as a read-along activity for small groups. These, too, help move children toward the goal of fluent, phrased reading and are invaluable for supporting ESL learners.
- Matching word cards and sentence strips helps children focus on visual information, as they tell each other different ways they can check to be sure the print is the same in the text as on the card or strip.
- Having children cover a few words in a text and write new words that fit the meaning and structure of the original text gives them experience with cross-checking. As new words are written and checked to see that they look right, all cue systems come into play.
- Sequencing the text and pictures of a well-known book gives children a structured retelling experience that makes them draw on information from all cueing systems. They must understand

the meaning of the book to get the pictures into correct order. Sequencing the text requires knowledge about whether or not the syntax, the flow of language, sounds right and makes sense. Graphophonic information helps them confirm particular words.

- Making available smaller copies of big books in book boxes provides additional resources for independent reading.

Using Shared Reading with Upper Elementary Students

Although often thought of as a teaching procedure only for younger children, shared reading can be used effectively across all grade levels. Nonfiction books in the content areas of science, social studies, and mathematics, as well as plays, songs, poems, and stories, enable teachers to demonstrate and to engage older learners in the content, language, and language structures of different text types. (Some specific examples are provided in Chapter 7.) Often, shared reading with upper-grade children is done with smaller groups. This allows for more focused input from individuals while maintaining the benefits of the social learning provided by a group.

Used with older children, shared reading can provide valuable opportunities for oral language development as well as models for reading, writing, and spelling.

Using Shared Reading with ESL Learners

For ESL students, shared reading provides a safe, nurturing environment where they can take part in nonthreatening experiences in their new language. Books and posters with poems, songs, and chants immerse children with language as it is used in an enjoyable way. They are able to listen, watch, and join in where they can and feel the personal satisfaction and enjoyment reading can bring. Because they are given the time and opportunity to return to the resources for rereading, the experiences build on one another, widening and deepening their experience with the new language and concepts.

The generous size of the pictures and print make the shared reading resources accessible and comprehensible. Mime, facial expressions, gestures, and dramatization provide further contextual support and make the new language understandable.

Patterned and predictable language structures and content are particularly helpful. So also are nonfiction books, which often reflect content that children have experienced for themselves. The use of photographs in these books make them much more easy to comprehend than some of the more abstract illustrations used to illustrate other kinds of books.

Using Shared Reading for Assessment

Shared reading provides countless opportunities for ongoing assessment. By closely observing two or three children each day, teachers can amass valuable information about attitudes, behaviors, skills, and strategies. The assessment takes place in the course of the shared reading experience and requires no preparation other than good "kidwatching" skills and knowledge of the reading process. Children's understanding of book and print conventions; their application of prior knowledge and experience; their use of cueing systems, either alone or in an integrated way; and comprehension—all can be observed and documented each day.

Working with Narrative Texts

The focus must be on ways in which the author encourages readers to feel as if their hands are on the author's pen, confident of the direction the story is most likely to follow.

Margaret Mooney

Every day we read for a range of purposes from an ever changing range of texts.

In the first two hours of this weekend morning, for example, I have already read the "use by" date on a carton of milk, glanced at the headlines of the local newspaper, read my favorite cartoon and the weather forecast, read and responded to my e-mail, checked the tennis results from Wimbledon on the Internet, and finished reading the final chapter of a novel. For each of these tasks I varied the way I read according to my purpose and the type of text. As an experienced reader, I do this without conscious effort.

Each text type has its own characteristics and makes its own demands of readers. Becoming familiar with these characteristics gives readers a powerful source of prediction. This in turn supports rapid processing of text and fluency. Shared reading is a perfect vehicle for introducing and involving children in a range of text types. This chapter discusses how to work with narrative texts in shared reading; the next chapter discusses informational texts.

Narrative texts most closely resemble the stories that children have experienced at home or in classroom read-aloud sessions. They are a powerful way of getting children "hooked on books." For this to happen, teachers must try to infuse the same involvement and enjoyment into the classroom reading as they do with their own personal reading for pleasure. The children should get inside the stories, predicting possible outcomes, empathizing with and taking on roles of the characters, reveling in the richness of language and the meanings it conveys. It is also important to get them hooked on authors and illustrators, as this gives them another level of understanding and enjoyment of the books.

Shared reading of narrative texts, such as *Jessie's Flower* (Bacon 1997), *Rat-a-tat-tat* (Eggleton 1997), *Crocodile Tea* (Vaughan 1997), and *The Royal Dinner* (Parkes 1990), encourages the children to:

- think and act like readers
- make connections across and between texts
- make connections with life and texts
- learn about plots, characters, settings, and themes
- experience a range of language and concepts
- think like authors and illustrators
- orchestrate the cueing systems

In the following example, Ms. Fisher is about to introduce a book about frogs to a group of ESL kindergarten children in the second week of school. The children live in a small farming community. To heighten interest in the book and to encourage children to talk with her about it, she has clipped heavy paper over the front cover.

Ms. Fisher: Can you tell me what this book is about, or do you need more information?
Brenna: Yes. Please more information.
(*The teacher tears off a portion of the paper.*)
Rosario (*excitedly pointing*): A tail! A tail!
Angy: Look! Look! Green beans!
Jerry: More information, please.
Ryan: A frog! It's green.
Ms. Fisher: What part of a frog is this?
Rosario: A leg.

Ms. Fisher (*peeling back the paper to show the entire frog*): What do you see? Tell me what you see.
Chorus: Frogs.

The teacher explains how pictures help cue meaning. Then she has the children visualize a frog they have seen and tell about it.

Ms. Fisher: Why do you think the frogs in this book are different colors?
Joey: So they can hide.
Ms. Fisher: What did you say? That's an awesome thought.
Joey (*pointing to frog*): They can hide.
Ms. Fisher: Where could this brown frog hide?
Ryan: In the dirt.
Rosario: In the leaves.
Ms. Fisher: And this orange one?
Angy: In an orange flower.
Ms. Fisher: Where could this green bullfrog hide?
Jerry: In the grass.
Brenna: In a lettuce. Or a cabbage.
Ms. Fisher: We call that camouflage.

When the story is over, the teacher invites the children to draw and write about a frog hiding (see Figure 6.1).

In this introduction, the teacher has supported the children to:

- think and act like readers
- make connections with life and texts
- experience a range of language and concepts
- think like authors and illustrators
- notice details in print and pictures

Working with Plot

The children should be encouraged to think about the text before, during, and after the reading. Questions to initiate dialogue might include:

- What do you think the story is going to be about?
- How did the pictures help you understand what was going on?

the frog likes flowers.

the frog is hiding in the grass.

Figure 6.1

- What part of the story did you like best? Why? Has anything like that ever happened to you?

Activities to reinforce the story line could include the following:

- drawing pictures to create a wall story for retellings
- dramatizing the story
- creating a flow diagram to document the action

Working with Characters

Questions to initiate dialogue about characters might include these:

- What would you tell a friend about this character?
- Did the character do anything that surprised you?
- Have you ever met anyone who was like this character?
- How has the illustrator helped you to know about the character?
- Which character would you like to be if we acted out the story?

Activities to help children focus on characterization include:

- drawing characters
- writing thought bubbles for characters
- writing dialogue for characters
- writing words to describe characters
- making a web to show how particular characters act
- creating masks and other props for dramatization of the story

Working with Setting

Questions to initiate dialogue about the setting of the story might include these:

- Where is this story happening?
- What would it be like to live in that place? What would you see? What could you do?
- How would the story change if it were in a different setting?

Activities to help children focus on setting include:

- drawing the setting
- changing the setting

Traditional Tales

Traditional tales, such as *The Three Little Pigs*, *Goldilocks*, and *The Little Red Hen*, share features that make them highly predictable, memorable stories. They are an excellent resource for encouraging emergent and early readers to think and act as readers and writers as they enjoy the predictable story lines and rhythmic language. The following features are what make traditional tales so useful for young readers:

- The plot is usually simple and fast moving with a clearly defined beginning, middle, and end.
- Characters and setting are usually established in the first paragraph.
- Language features such as rhyme, rhythm, repetition, and the use of onomatopoeia and alliteration make the stories memorable and provide many places for children to join in.
- The characters' actions are highly predictable.

Shared reading and writing with traditional tales provides children with the opportunity to work with these special features.

Spotlight on Visual Features

In addition to the features just mentioned, many versions of traditional tales or folktales use special print features to draw children's attention to memorable parts of the language and events. Repetitive refrains are often written in colored, enlarged, or bold print, which makes them easy to recognize and remember. These kinds of tales are among the first texts that children consistently join in reading.

When the print relates to an exciting event or a high point it is often enlarged or specially formatted to add dramatic effect and support expressive reading and, of course, to provide another toehold or entry point for young readers. Figure 6.2, from *Goldilocks and the Three Bears* (Hillman 1989), is an example of how text can be highlighted.

Sometimes the print follows the direction of the action:

```
                   hills
        up           and                              down
    ran                       down                     the
  He                          hills.                          steps
```

The dialogue of different characters is frequently written in different colors, and often in a thick, bold font. This is particularly helpful for cueing the children to recognize and read character parts and provides teachers and children with an easy way to rewrite the book as a play.

Supportive Layouts

As can easily be seen in this example from the story of *The Little Red Hen*, the repetitive nature of traditional tales lends itself to print layouts that are highly supportive of young readers:

"Not I," grunted the pig.
"Not I," meowed the cat.
"Not I," quacked the duck.
"Not I," barked the dog.

Not only does this kind of layout provide easy access to reading, remembering, and understanding the print, it also provides a perfect setting for later teaching the concepts of one-to-one correspondence, the constancy of print, punctuation, or high-frequency words.

Memorable Language, Characters, and Action

The features of traditional tales combine to help children to take in meaning, language patterns, and language structures as well as vocabulary. In the example that follows, the teacher is working in a transition class of mostly Spanish-speaking children. As the teacher introduces the new story, *The Goat in the Chile Patch* (Kratky 1989), she uses many gestures and demonstrations of movement to help the children comprehend the language and meaning and to actively involve them. She begins by

They had three beds —
a **great big** bed
for Papa Bear,

a **middle-sized** bed
for Mama Bear,

and a teeny-weeny bed
for Baby Bear.

Figure 6.2

drawing the children's attention to the cover, which shows a goat with a chile in its mouth. She identifies Rigo, who is hoeing the chile patch, and talks about how he is feeling. She reads the narrator's text in her normal voice and uses different voices to introduce each character.

Teacher (*reading*): "One fine day, just like that (*she snaps her fingers to give meaning to the idiom*), a goat (*pointing to the illustration*) got into (*moving her finger to indicate how the goat moved from outside the fence to the other side*)—"
Children: The chile patch.
Teacher: The chile patch (*traces the outline of the patch*). (*Then, pointing to the illustration of Rigo, stamps her feet rapidly and waving her hand*) "Rigo ran to the goat. Get out! Get away!"

She continues to involve the children through graphic demonstrations that support meaning and invite their participation. Toward the end of the book, many children are already joining in for the repetitive parts of the story. All are eagerly waiting for the goat to meet his match.

Center and Small-Group Activities

Traditional tales are excellent texts to use for small-group and center work. When planning ways to use these resources, always make sure that the activities provide authentic purposes for reading and writing that also reflect the genre. The following ideas deepen children's understanding of the language, content, and structure of the books. These activities should always be demonstrated first in a group setting during shared reading time and used by children with teacher support before being used independently in small-group and center work. Each provides an explicit mini-lesson for a small group. Many of the ideas contain simple variations that can add to their complexity and extend their usefulness and appeal. All of the ideas here can be used by purchasing double copies of remaindered trade book versions of the same traditional tale as the shared book version. I am always on the lookout for these at book sales. I laminate them to help ensure that they can take years of wear, but also (and more importantly) to enable children to write on them with erasable markers. I store the activities in labeled zippered plastic bags together with a small version of the classroom big book.

Focus on Plot

Here is an activity that is excellent for reinforcing the sequence of beginning, middle, and end.

Demonstrate this activity to the children by first rereading the big book or recalling the story through discussion. Distribute sequence picture cards to pairs of children. Ask the pair who has the first picture to hold it up and tell how they know it is the first. When the others in the group agree it is the first picture, have the pair tell that part of the story. Continue this way until all the pictures are sequenced in the right order. In their retelling, encourage the children to use the language of the story.

Using Sequence Pictures for Retelling
This activity can also be done by children on their own. Here's how:

1. Collect two trade book copies of a different version of your traditional tale big book.
2. Cut out the illustrations and discard the written text.
3. Laminate the illustrations.
4. Place the illustrations in a zippered plastic bag with a small book copy of the big book version of the story.
5. Have the children use the small book as reference for sequencing the new illustrations and retelling the story.

Changing the Challenge

Here is a variation on the basic sequencing activity, which may be used once the children can sequence the pictures and tell the story. Write a simple version of the shared book on laminated cards. Add these cards to the container for students to sequence both illustrations and text. Then, after a while, add a new challenge by removing two of the illustrations and replacing them with blank laminated cards. Have the children draw the missing illustrations.

As a further variation to this sequencing activity, remove the first and last text cards and replace them with blank laminated cards for children to write missing text.

To increase the challenge still further, replace *all* the text cards with blank laminated cards and invite the children to write a complete retelling of the story.

This final activity could be modeled with the children's active input during shared or interactive writing over a few days. The completed story could be displayed on the classroom wall as a model for the activity as well as a resource for other reading and writing.

Stretch the Story

Another variation on the sequencing activity invites children to go beyond the content of the book to create an additional event. This activity should already have been modeled through the class's writing an innovation on a text. For instance, they could introduce a new character in place of the Gingerbread Man, or in the story of Goldilocks and the Three Bears they might write what the bears or Goldilocks did next.

1. Distribute the segments of a traditional tale to the group, but include two blank cards with them.
2. The group sequences the text and decides where they wish to put the blanks.

3. As a group, the children write or draw the additional text.
4. They then read the whole new story to make sure it is coherent and makes sense.

Focus on Story Characters and Language

Because traditional tales are peopled by larger-than-life characters, they provide wonderful opportunities for children to write descriptions. In addition, the memorable language many of the characters use makes an excellent resource for drawing children's attention to the visual features of print with familiar text.

Who Said That?

The activities here require very little teacher preparation. I make multiple photocopies of illustrations of the characters I want to use and invite the children to color them. Then I laminate the pages as well as some dialogue bubbles and descriptions and store them in bags with a small copy of the class big book, and the package is ready for use.

This first activity focuses children's attention on visual features of print and one-to-one matching.

1. Provide illustrations of characters from traditional stories.
2. Make dialogue bubbles containing well-known sayings such as "Fe, fi, fo, fum" or "Then I'll do it myself."
3. Students match the dialogue bubbles to the characters.

Changing the Challenge

You may increase the challenge of this activity by putting the children in the second character's shoes and having them think of a suitable reply. This activity combines inferencing as well as practice in both oral and written language.

I Say, I Say

Here is an alternative activity using the same materials:

1. Provide illustrations of two storybook characters.
2. Add dialogue bubbles for each character.
3. Provide the language for one dialogue bubble; leave the other bubble blank.

4. Have students reread the small book and then write the character's reply.

What Did They Say?

This task asks children to substitute new dialogue for existing text or to draw inferences from the pictures and write appropriate dialogue. The activity is enhanced by having children work in pairs, so that each can assume a character part and try out different dialogue that makes sense before writing it down.

1. Provide illustrations of story characters from some active point in the story.
2. Add empty dialogue bubbles.
3. Have students write appropriate dialogue for each character.
4. Then ask the group to read the different versions to each other.

What Did They Think?

As a variation to the What Did They Say? activity, provide thought bubbles for one or two characters in an illustration. Then ask questions, such as: What is the Gingerbread Man thinking as he runs away? What is Jack thinking as he leads his cow down the road to be sold? What is the fisherman thinking as he returns to ask the fish for yet another wish? This activity helps children to read between the lines and supports their ability to make inferences.

What Do They Look Like?

Other activities can give children practice writing descriptions. This helps them focus their attention on the role of illustrations in traditional tales, the details contained in the illustrations, and the different ways illustrators portray characters.

1. Provide illustrations of two traditional characters.
2. Add descriptive words or statements about each character's appearance.
3. Have students match appropriate words to characters.
4. Provide several blank laminated cards for students to write further descriptions.

What I Did

Here's another activity focusing on description:

1. Provide illustrations of several traditional characters.
2. Write statements describing their actions.
3. Have students match appropriate statements to characters.
4. Provide several blank laminated cards for students to write other appropriate statements.

While all these activities can be used with children at levels K–3, they can also be used with upper elementary children who could benefit from using the structure of the tales in their own writing. They also provide powerful scaffolding for ESL students.

Reinforcing High-Frequency Words

Activities can also be developed to help children learn about high-frequency words. For example:

1. Provide a big book and a packet of high-frequency words that appear in the story.
2. Have the children read the story in pairs or small groups; then have them match the high-frequency words to those in the story.

Working with Upper Elementary Students

Traditional tales have much to offer upper elementary students as well as younger learners. Different versions of traditional tales are found across cultures, making them excellent resources for comparing how different authors develop setting, plot, and characterization and ways illustrators depict them. In our increasingly diverse classrooms these stories also validate the experiences and perspectives of others, building bridges across different languages and cultures.

The books also help children maintain meaning and build momentum over longer stretches of continuous text. This supports the development of phrasing and fluency for less experienced older readers. The clear-cut structure of these texts is also useful for teaching text structure, particularly the concept of beginning, middle, and end. Not only does this provide a framework to support retelling and writing, it also builds experience. In addition, it can be an authentic test preparation activity when children are called upon to recall sequences of events and identify a text's beginning, middle, and end. Finally, narrative texts can provide opportunities for many response activities. For example, children may be asked to consider the point of view of characters, such as the Troll in *Three Billy Goats Gruff*; write newspaper reports; or create character descriptions and dramatizations.

7

Informational Texts

Pupils are to become part of the shared and sharing thinking which not only gives them access to knowledge but also lets them create and interpret it because it has become alive for them.

Margaret Meek

Informational texts make up a large and rapidly growing part of our everyday reading. Lists, road signs, TV guides, ATMs, e-mail, advertising, and store signs are just a few of the texts we routinely read as we go about our lives. In the workplace, too, the kinds of information we need to use and understand are proliferating at a rapid rate.

Young children begin informational texts at an early age. Environmental print, or logo reading is among the first kinds of written material preschoolers ascribe meaning to as they recognize the symbols that stand for things and places that are important in their lives. Well before they enter school they are able to confidently name banks, stores, fast food outlets, road signs, and other familiar, recognizable print. Despite the important role environmental print plays in the everyday lives of children and their families, until recently narrative text has been used almost exclusively to teach children to read.

Informational, or nonfiction, books should also be included in a balanced literacy program from the child's first days of school. As Christine Duthie (1996) reminds us these books "build on the literate encounters children have experienced long before they enter school."

The benefits of including nonfiction books in the K–2 literacy program are considerable. Children find the real-world topics, with the photographs frequently used to illustrate them, interesting and accessible. Because the books feature real places, people, things, and events, they are often easier to relate to and understand than fantasy topics. They allow children to draw on their prior knowledge and experience to make meaning. The introduction of nonfiction reading and writing in the early years also builds a foundation for later reading in the content areas and for lifelong learning. Hoyt (1999) adds, "Informational texts that are predictable and well written provide emergent as well as developing and fluent readers with opportunities to apply their fledgling understandings about print while expanding their world knowledge" (p. 121).

Research by Armbruster et al. (1991) shows that much of the process of locating and understanding information in texts may be learned only, or may be learned best, through teacher and peer modeling and plenty of practice with diminishing amounts of scaffolding. Shared reading offers a powerful way to accomplish this teaching and learning in a meaningful, purposeful way. By using resources that reflect the content areas, teachers can also integrate and support literacy teaching across the curriculum.

To become effective readers of informational texts students need to understand:

- the features that identify nonfiction books
- the selective way nonfiction is read according to the reader's purpose
- the ways organizational features such as indexes, contents pages, glossaries, and headings help the reader access a text
- the specialized language and language structures used to convey information
- how visual literacy such as photographs, diagrams, maps, and charts combine with the written text to convey information
- how information in captions and labels combines with running text to convey information
- strategies for using prior knowledge and experience to engage in inquiry with texts

For many children, nonfiction opens the door to seeing a purpose for reading. As they use nonfiction resources to pursue their personal interests and hobbies, books and reading become an integral part of their lives, both in and out of the classroom.

I always include nonfiction books in the read-aloud component of my balanced literacy program and make sure they are readily available for rereading and browsing, and as references for the children to use in their own writing and drawing. In kindergarten and first grade, many of the children's favorites come from the Candlewick Press Read and Wonder Series. These beautiful books combine superb illustrations and high-interest stories and poems with nonfiction text and ideas. The nonfiction component is clearly separated from the story but cleverly weaves in facts and questions that support and extend the story information. The books invite children's active involvement and help to lay a strong foundation for thinking and questioning. Another wonderful nonfiction book for first and second grades is Jonathan London's *Voices of the Wild.* The language, imagery, and illustrations combine to make this a powerful introductory experience to the craft of nonfiction writing.

In addition to reading aloud, I like to use several carefully selected shared reading books to demonstrate that nonfiction can be a source of pleasure as well as information. The children and I spend several days browsing through these texts and exploring their special features through a combination of talking, thinking, looking, and reading.

One of my personal favorites for involving young children as readers of informational texts is *Beavers* (Moore 1996). The book is beautifully illustrated, has just the right amount of text, and provides a rich context for children to ask and seek answers to questions. Each day, we choose a few pages from the table of contents and dip into the text for further exploration of the topic. The following excerpts detail some of our discussions:

Teacher: This book about beavers is one of my favorites, and I think you will enjoy it too. (*Pointing*) What does the cover illustration tell you about them?

Tim: It shows what they look like.

Teacher: Yes. It does. How would you describe a beaver to someone who had never seen one? What would you say?

Tim: I'd say it was kinda small . . . and real hairy.

Teacher: Can you think of something about the same size to compare it with?

Ann: It looks about the same size as a groundhog . . .

Harry: The illustration shows where they live.

Amie: It shows what they do too. Look (*pointing*). You can see where it has just cut down that tree . . .

After discussion about why the beavers choose their particular habitat and how they build their lodges I turn to the back cover. I explain the role of a blurb, and we read the information together and share what we already know about the questions the blurb poses. Next we read the title page. The children comment on the picture of the mother and baby beavers. No one knows what these babies are called, and we hope the text will tell us.

Teacher: How can we find out if the book tells about the baby beavers?
Mike: We can check the table of contents.
Teacher: Let's read it together.

We read the table of contents and decide that we might find the answer to our question in the section "Beaver Family Life." The illustrations we find there quickly confirm that our choice is right. I use this opportunity to demonstrate how to skim and scan the print to locate information about the kits. Because the topic has really caught the children's interest, we read the four pages about family life and discuss the information provided by the illustrations.

The next day we choose to read the section on pages 5–8 headed "What Is a Beaver?" The opening text reads:

> Have you ever seen a porcupine, a gray squirrel, or a deer mouse? If you have, then you have seen one of the cousins of the beaver. (pp. 4–5)

This double-page spread provides fertile ground for discussion as we discuss the features these creatures share with the beaver. This focuses the children's attention on details in the illustrations and provides the opportunity for them to draw inferences based on that information.

Ann: They all have the same kind of fur.
Tim: They all use trees to live.
Teacher: What do you mean, Tim?
Tim: The squirrels live up the tree. They climb up to escape their enemies. The squirrels and mice get food from the trees, and the beaver cuts down trees to make the lodge.
Teacher: Good thinking, Tim. There could be more information on the next pages . . .

We read together and find that these animals are all rodents. The text defines what a rodent is, and I use this opportunity to point out how the author crafts a definition.

The following day we read the pages that explain why beavers gnaw. I use this opportunity to have the children set a purpose for reading by having them scan the text and identify the words that tell what they want to know. Another strategy has been demonstrated.

Over the next few days we return to the text to think, read, look, and discuss content. By the time we finish the book I have been able to implicitly model and engage children in a wide range of nonfiction strategies and behaviors. During the next few weeks I continue to choose other information-rich texts to share in the same way.

When the children have had time to absorb a good deal of information about how nonfiction texts work I begin to explicitly model and engage children in using these strategies.

Identifying Nonfiction Books

To teach children in kindergarten and grade 1 how fiction and nonfiction differ, I display the covers of several fiction books alongside a nonfiction one. I make sure ahead of time that the nonfiction book contains photographs and a contents page and that its subject is some real object or event the children might be familiar with. I ask the children to look at the covers of the displayed books and to scan through their pages to identify which books are fiction and which nonfiction, and tell how they know. We repeat this activity with several more sets of books to ensure that the children have ample opportunity for browsing and discussion.

As we look at the books we identify the features that define nonfiction texts, such as:

- real people, places, objects, events
- photographs
- diagrams and maps
- captions and labels
- table of contents, glossary, index
- headings

We make a chart listing the differences between fiction and nonfiction.

Fiction Books
- are make-believe
- tell stories about imaginary people and places
- often use illustrations

Nonfiction Books
- are true
- give information about real people and places
- often use photographs and diagrams

We use the chart as an ongoing reference and continue to add information as the children find out more about nonfiction.

Setting a Purpose for Reading

Children must learn the importance of setting a purpose for their reading and understand how this affects the way they read. In this second-grade classroom the teacher is introducing the high-interest big book *As Big as a Whale* from Newbridge's Ranger Rick series. Before they begin reading, he asks, "What do you know about this topic?" As the children volunteer information, he records their responses on Post-it notes and attaches these to a white board.

migrate
mammals
flukes
blowholes
tail fins
eat plankton
many kinds
blue whales
calves
toothed whales
humpbacks
sing
hold breath
baleen whales
eat small fish
orcas

Then he works with the children to sort and classify the information into related groups.

Kinds	Food	Body Parts	Other
humpback	plankton	blowholes	mammals
blue whales	small fish	flukes	migrate
baleen whales		tail fins	sing
toothed whales			calves
orcas			hold breath

When the children are satisfied with their classifications the teacher asks, "What do you want to find out about whales?" To help the children formulate their questions, he reminds them to use the words *how*, *when*, *what*, *why*, and *where*. He and the children discuss the questions, and then he helps them choose two questions they want the book to answer. He writes these on a chart. He tells the children it is important to choose the best way to read the text in order to achieve their purpose. They brainstorm the choices:

- Skim to get an understanding of the content.
- Scan to locate specific information.
- Reread to confirm meaning, check understanding, and crystallize details.

The children decide to skim the text first, to see if the questions are likely to be answered; if they are, the children will scan for specific information.

Together they skim the table of contents and identify a likely chapter. They proceed to skim, then scan the text of the chapter to locate information that answers their questions. They follow up by rereading to clarify their understanding. As he completes the lesson the teacher continues to model the inquiry process by having children reflect on:

- what they have learned
- how they have learned it
- how this fits with their existing knowledge
- what their questions are now

Over the next few days the class returns to the book to seek answers to new questions and to practice skimming, scanning, and rereading to locate, read, and comprehend the information. The shared reading acts as a catalyst for shared and guided writing and independent center work.

Using a Table of Contents

Using a table of contents to locate information quickly and effectively is an essential nonfiction skill. For K–1 children I like to begin our exploration by displaying a table of contents and asking the group the following questions:

- What is this?
- Why do you think the author wrote it?

Discussion in response to these questions establishes that the purpose of the contents page is to tell the reader what information is in the book and the page numbers where they will find the information.

Together, the children and I then survey a number of books to find different ways authors write contents pages and to practice using them to locate information. We compile the information onto a large chart as a reference for their own writing. Of course, we leave room so that we may continue to add to our chart.

All About Contents Pages
Pictograms (show photocopy example)
Solid lines between words and numerals
Dotted lines between words and numerals
Chronological organization

We talk about the difference between the way readers use a table of contents in a fiction book and in a nonfiction book. In a fiction book the chapters must be read in order, whereas in a nonfiction book the reader can often "dip in" and read sections in any order.

The following day we choose one of the nonfiction books and practice using the contents page to find specific information. We:

1. read the contents page together
2. work in pairs to read an entry in the table of contents and find the page number
3. speculate on the information we might find in that section
4. locate the pages
5. read the section together the first time to gain a general understanding of the content

6. read it again for a specific purpose, such as to find a fact or definition
7. repeat the process

Using Headings

Often the children and I explore headings at the same time as they learn to use a contents page. However, I always devote several lessons explicitly to the role of headings in nonfiction books. The following lesson in grade 1 focuses on how the heading tells the reader what is going to be in the subsequent text.

1. We read some entries in the table of contents.
2. We match the table of contents topics to the headings and discuss how authors use boldface, italics, or other distinctive print to make the headings stand out.
3. Next we read two or three headings and the text that follows each. We discuss how effective the heading was in helping us predict and understand the content.
4. After this I cover a heading and we read the text that follows it. Together we compose a heading that we feel best describes the content. Then we uncover the author's heading and compare it with ours.

As a follow-up to this activity, we select a book that has no headings but does have very clear-cut content. Over several days, we read sections of this text and compose headings to describe it. We write these on Post-it notes that we attach to the book. Finally, we use the headings during a shared writing session to compile a contents page for the book.

Using an Index

When children are able to use a table of contents easily, I introduce another organizational tool: the index. I show the children that an index helps readers find more specific information than the contents page can. It also lists the information in alphabetical order. A typical explicit lesson on indexes in grade 2 generally follows a format like this:

1. Raise a specific question the children want an informational book to answer.
2. Skim the contents page for relevant information.
3. Now check the index to show how it pinpoints the information.
4. Use the page numbers indicated in the index to find and read the specific content.
5. Have children write or draw what they found out.

Reading and Comprehending Specialized Language

Results from standardized tests and research, Pearson and Fielding (1991) show children experience difficulty searching for information in nonfiction texts. This is not surprising, considering the small amount of time children spend learning to read these kinds of texts.

The following example from Mr. Lomas's classroom shows how he uses the book *Investigating Your Backyard* (Lunis 1999) to help children identify, pronounce, and comprehend specialized language. Figure 7.1, which reproduces pages 8 and 9, is typical of the way the information is presented in this book.

Mr. Lomas: What does the cover help you know?
Tom: The title says "Investigating Your Backyard." Maybe the boy thinks he's an investigator.
Megan: Yeah. He's looking real carefully at the butterfly.
Mr. Lomas: What do you think he could find out by observing the butterfly?
Sonia: Its colors and stuff.
Megan: Where it lives. What it eats.
Mr. Lomas: Maybe. If he likes finding out about bugs, what kind of scientist would he be called? (*Silence*) This book describes different backyard scientists and what they do. Let's take a look at the contents page and the introduction and choose some pages to read.

He reads these with the help of the children, and they choose pages 6 and 7 to read (see Figure 2.1 in Chapter 2, which reproduces page 6).

Mr. Lomas: Let's skim-read to see what kind of scientist she is.
Chas: A bot-a-nist. Botanist. Are the names of the scientists always in green print in this book?

No matter where you live, you should be able to find insects all around you. If you are fascinated by these tiny, six-legged creatures, you can call yourself a backyard entomologist (en-tuh-MOL-uh-jist).

There are many different kinds of insects. Compare the insects in the photos. How are they alike? How are they different?

Ground Beetle

Cricket

Ladybugs

Figure 7.1

Mr. Lomas: Yes. That helps readers find the special words quickly. See how this pronunciation guide after the word helps you to know how to say the word? Let's try to do it. (*He articulates the word* botanist, *pointing to each section of the word as he does.*) Now let's look at the text and check the picture and find out what a botanist is.

Tom: A scientist who studies plants.

Mr. Lomas: Let's highlight those words. (*He does so with removable highlighter tape.*) Now let's read the special word, the pronunciation guide, and the definition and see how it all fits together.

He asks the children to scan the print to find out what questions botanists ask. The children read and discuss the information and questions on page 7. Mr. Lomas then reads through the next few pages with the students, having them first identify the name of each scientist and then following the pronunciation guide before highlighting the definition of each scientist with the tape. Mr. Lomas draws the lesson to an end by having the children summarize their learning.

Mr. Lomas: What did you notice about the way the author gave you information about words you might not have heard before?

Chas: She wrote them in a color so they are easy to find.

Sarah: She showed us how to pronounce them.

Zoe: And she always told us straight away what they meant.

Rico: Sometimes she told us before the word and sometimes she told us later.

Mr. Lomas: Good thinking. You all know a lot about how nonfiction writers organize their writing to help you read and understand it.

Rico: We could use that in our own writing too.

In this lesson children have been supported to:

- draw on information in the title and cover
- relate prior knowledge and experience
- set a purpose for their reading
- integrate information from print and photographs
- use a contents page to locate information
- skim to obtain an overall picture
- scan to locate specific information
- learn how specialized language is often defined immediately before or after the word
- use a pronunciation guide

Shared reading from an overhead transparency is another way to teach these strategies, with highlighter pens used to identify relationships between the various pieces of information.

Noticing Detail in Pictures

Many nonfiction books that are written for K–2 readers use large photographs and insets with minimal text to convey information. This requires children to interpret a great deal of information from the photographs and to recognize relationships between them.

In the following example, Mr. Paul demonstrates how a reader carries out detailed examinations of pictures by using double-page spreads like the one shown in Figure 7.2, pages 4 and 5 of *The Rain Forest* (Cory 1998). He begins by reading the running text and discussing how it

The top level, or canopy, is thick with leaves and branches. From above, it looks like a green blanket.

Many animals find all they need to survive here without going down to the ground.

passion-vine butterfly

Figure 7.2

matches the main picture. Then he invites the children to look carefully at the insets. They discuss how the inset photographs extend the information and what inferences they can draw from them.

Gemma: I know something (*pointing*). Look. The little photos show that different kinds of creatures live there.

Mr. Paul: They certainly do! What creatures do we see here?

Mica: An eagle.

Verona: And a monkey and a butterfly too. It's just come out of that thing!

Mr. Paul: So it has. It has just hatched from its chrysalis. Let's focus on looking at the butterfly. Look at the picture closely and see how the butterfly can survive without going down to the ground.

Gemma: It can fly with its wings. It can rest on the leaves or the branches when it gets tired.

Rae: And it can shelter under the leaves when it rains.

Mica: How will it get food?

Verona: Some of the trees might have flowers. Butterflies could get nectar from the flowers.

Mica: The butterfly can lay its eggs on the leaves too.

Mr. Paul: So the butterfly can survive without going down to the ground. Now what does the photo tell you about the eagle?

Gemma: It has huge wings to fly and look for food and shelter.

Verona: And strong claws to hang on to the branches.

Sue: It can catch food in its claws…

Gemma: Would the eagle eat the butterfly?

Following the discussion, the children help Mr. Paul write the information on a chart.

Tamarin	**Eagle**	**Butterfly**
Sharp claws help it climb.	Huge wings help it fly.	Lays eggs on leaves.
Might make a home in a hole in a tree.	Strong claws help it catch food.	Gets shelter from leaves.

Integrating Information from Print and Diagrams

Diagrams are commonly used in nonfiction books to convey information. For example, Figure 7.3, which depicts page 4 from the book *Looking at Insects* (Glover 1998), can be used as part of an activity to help children read and understand a diagram and integrate the information with that written in the running text.

1. Read the contents page with the children to locate general information about insects.
2. Have them help find the page. Skim the page and discuss how the author has presented the information through headings, running text, and a labeled diagram.
3. After reading the running text, list the information it provides on a chart. Next, examine the details in the diagram and read the labels. Discuss how they confirm or extend the written text.
4. Alongside the list that details the information in the running text, make a list of the ways the diagram contributed to the meaning.

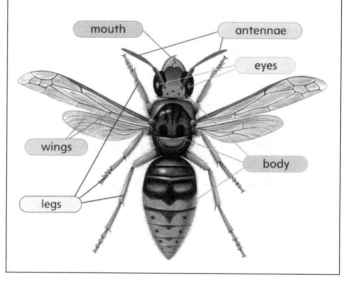

Figure 7.3

In this kind of lesson, the children are supported to:

- use a contents page
- read running text
- list information
- examine diagrams

- recall, check, and record information
- compare information

Introducing Diagrams and Labels

Labels help readers understand what they are looking at in pictures and diagrams.

To introduce diagrams and labels to a kindergarten class, choose a big book that has large, uncluttered pictures and well-defined labels. (Excellent examples are included in the yellow and orange levels of Rigby's Discovery World.)

In the following example Ms. Shelley has chosen to use the book *Amazing Eggs* (Llewellyn 1998) from the Discovery World series to talk about labels and their purpose. This book features a large photograph and one to three lines of print on each page. The print is clearly separated from the picture. Each animal picture includes the name of the creature on a clear, easy-to-see label. There is nothing to distract children's attention.

Ms. Shelley: This book tells us about different kinds of animals who lay eggs. Let's turn the pages one by one and look at the pictures.
Bettina: What kinds of eggs are those?
Suzie: Chicken eggs.
Ms. Shelley (*pointing*): The author has used a label to tell us whose eggs they are. They are—
Suzie: Duck's eggs.
Ms. Shelley: Let's look at the pictures and labels on the next page. What does this label tell you?

To bring the lesson to a close, Ms. Shelley places a big book on the easel and opens it to a large, clear picture of a frog. She asks the children to name the body parts of the frog. She models how to label the parts by writing the name of each body part on a Post-it note and using a Wikki Stix™ to mark a line from the body part to the label (see Figure 7.4).

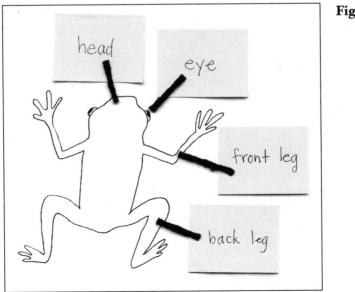

Figure 7.4

Reading Captions and Labels

Many nonfiction books feature captions and labels, yet often children do not realize that these convey important information. Indeed, research shows that in many instances they do not read them at all (Walpole 1999). The following lesson helps third-grade children see how captions help readers understand what they are looking at and how this information is integrated with the running text to provide meaning.

1. Cover the captions on one page of a nonfiction book.
2. Read the running text and discuss the information.
3. Examine the picture or diagram the caption describes and have children predict the content of the caption.
4. List their ideas.
5. Peel away the cover and read the caption.
6. Discuss how closely the children's predictions came to the actual caption.
7. Discuss how the caption enhanced their understanding of the picture.
8. Discuss how the caption added to the information in the running text.
9. Discuss how the caption helped them understand the text.

Using Prior Knowledge and Experience in a Book Introduction

Many kinds of prior knowledge affect children's ability to locate and understand information in nonfiction texts, including knowledge about the topic, organizational features of the text, and organizational patterns of the language. The following example from a second-grade classroom supports children's use of prior knowledge and comprehension in gathering information about the topic from the cover and contents page of a book.

In order to focus children's attention on the cover information, Ms. Roberts has fastened heavy paper over the front cover of a nonfiction book. She wants the children to notice details in the pictures and print and to understand how the two combine to provide information. The children are intrigued by the hidden cover and eager to find out why Ms. Roberts has covered it. They listen and watch closely as she introduces the book.

Ms. Roberts: We can get a lot of information about a book from the cover. We can find out what it might be about by looking at the photographs and the title. First I am going to show you the picture on the cover of this nonfiction book a little bit at a time. I want you to look for clues that help you think what it might be about. (*She tears off a small piece of paper to reveal a section of the picture.*)

Michael: I can see blue. It's the sea.

Gina: It could be space. It looks blue too.

Peta: Or it could be a lake like Lake Michigan.

Ms. Roberts: It could be any of these. Let's look at some more of the picture and get more information to help you.

Michael: I can see part of a diver's flipper. It is the sea.

Peta: It could still be a lake. Divers go in lakes too.

The children continue to modify their predictions as more of the picture is disclosed. Finally a whale is revealed.

Next, Ms. Roberts asks the children to predict what the title will be. They problem-solve from the print clues as she gradually reveals the title, *As Big as a Whale* (Berger 1996). She challenges the children to predict the possible content of the book based on the information in the title and cover picture.

Sean: It will probably compare the whale's size with other things.

Ms. Roberts: Why do you think that?

Sean: The word *big* in the title. It might say some things are bigger and some are smaller.

Ms. Roberts: I like the way you used that information.

Mario: There'll be something about different kinds of whales too.

Ms. Roberts: There could be. Where can we look to check what topics the author has written about?

Sean: The contents page.

Ms. Roberts: Will you find it for me, please?

They read the table of contents and check their predictions. There is no specific reference to the size of whales in the contents page, but there is in the introduction on the facing page.

Ms. Roberts: Look, Sean. The introduction talks about sizes. (*Sean beams happily as the teacher reads*) "The blue whale is the biggest animal that ever lived. It is as long as three buses, as heavy as 25 elephants, and as tall as a two-story building."

After a brief discussion, Ms. Roberts asks the children to read the table of contents again and to choose the topic they would like to read about. In this lesson, the children have:

- used prior knowledge and experience to predict from print and pictures and justify their predictions
- self-monitored to check and confirm their predictions
- had the use of a contents page identified and modeled
- used the contents-page information to locate and read relevant text

Learning to Locate Information

Children need to learn strategies for effectively locating specific information. Working in small groups, choose a question the children have identified from an earlier reading of a big book. Distribute an array of trade books or related big books and ask them to identify the best ones to look in to find the answer. Give them time to skim and scan the books. When they have made their selection, ask them to justify it to the group.

Teacher: Why did you choose that book, Cam?
Cam: There's a little bit of information on the back of the book. It says . . . (*Cam reads the blurb to the group*).
Peggy: I looked at the covers and found two books that help with the question.
Murphy: The contents page and the index in this book have a heap of information . . .
Reagan: This one has a great diagram . . .

Have the children narrow the selection to the four or five books that best answer the question. List the information the children find before helping them synthesize it to form an answer to the question in their own words. Then, compile a chart with the children to help remind them of ways to locate information. Mr. Maxwell and his class came up with this:

Looking for information?

You can:

- skim the contents page
- scan the index
- read the blurb
- read the title and look at the cover picture
- read the author
- read the publisher

8

Innovating on Shared Reading Books: The Reading-Writing Connection

The children respond with a delighted feeling of authorship, enjoying the opportunity for a genuinely personal and creative experience yet supported by the familiar structure.

Don Holdaway

Because reading and writing are closely linked (Clay 1998; Hansen 1987), shared reading books can be as valuable a writing resource as they are for reading. They readily lend themselves to innovation, providing powerful scaffolds, or frameworks, for children to think and act like writers in collaborative situations. As the children carry out writing decisions, they are also engaged in powerful work with phonemic awareness and phonics. Innovating on a known text extends what young writers can do and allows older writers the chance to experience success over longer stretches of writing. The books children themselves plan, write, and illustrate become classroom favorites, and the shared writing experience stays with them as a powerful model for independent writing.

Of course, innovations are only one of the kinds of writing experience available to children in a balanced literacy program. Interactive, shared, and guided writing allow them to continue to build on their knowledge and experience as writers. Children should also be given the freedom and time to write for their own purposes about topics of their own choice.

What are the purposes and benefits of innovating on texts?

- It puts the pen in the reader's hand.
- It demonstrates the reading-writing connection.
- It engages children in thinking like an author.
- It sets a purpose for reading, comprehending, and composing.
- It establishes a scaffold for sustained writing.
- It supplies wonderful classroom resources for shared reading.
- It builds oral language.
- It focuses children's thinking on meaning, structure, layout, print, and pictures and other visual supports such as diagrams, maps, and cutaways.
- It creates authentic purposes for phonemic awareness, phonics, and spelling.

In addition to this, innovations provide children with powerful models for engaging with and practicing many of the tasks they must encounter in state and national tests. Common test assignments include recognizing the beginning, middle, and end of a narrative; finding the main idea; drawing inferences; understanding characterization and point of view; reshaping the content of informational texts; interpreting pictures, maps, and other visual text; and translating written text into webs, charts, and diagrams. All of these can be modeled and engaged in during the authentic, whole-text experience of innovating on a shared book.

Innovations on single words are an effective way to begin. In the following example the children have decided to replace the word *jump* in this repetitive refrain from *Goodnight, Goodnight* (Parkes 1989).

Jump on my bed
and join the fun.
There's lots of room
for everyone!

They begin by brainstorming a list of possible replacements. After choosing the word, the teacher covers *jump* and, with the children's help, writes in the new word.

Mr. Wolski: Listen as I say the word. What letter does *hop* begin with?
Alissa: *H.*
Mr. Wolski: Will it be a big *H* or a small *h*?
Clem: Big, 'cause it starts a sentence.
Mr. Wolski (*as he writes the* H): Good thinking. *H-op.* What do I need to write next? What sounds do you hear as I say *op*?

When the word is written they read their "new" refrain.

Hop on my bed
and join the fun...

The refrain occurs several times in the book. The children find and change all the *jumps* to *hop* for consistency and meaning.

In this simple innovation the children have:

- identified words that make sense and sound right (semantics and syntax)
- listened closely to the sounds that make up the word (phonemic awareness)
- matched sounds to letters (graphophonics)

Innovations need not be elaborate. Indeed, many of the most effective and engaging innovations are made with very few and very simple changes to the original book. The example shown in Figure 8.1, from a group of kindergarteners, is one of my favorites. The original book features a cast of farm animals. They are peeping, one by one, at cutout clues on the pages to discover the identity of a mysterious creature who has been put into a shed in the dead of the night. The children have replaced the animal characters with pictures of themselves and have used their own names in the text. They have changed the creature in the shed to a ghost. The last page of their book shows their rapidly retreating feet around the edges of the page. Charming and highly engaging, the book overflows with their ownership and pride.

In the following, more elaborate example, a group of second graders has decided to write an innovation on *Goodnight, Goodnight.* This book

Figure 8.1

features storybook and nursery-rhyme characters joining in a nighttime romp with a little girl and her teddy bear (see Chapter 4). The book has many predictable features in the language and illustrations to invite the readers into the text, including:

- well-known nursery-rhyme and folktale characters
- language associated with those characters
- picture clues and language clues to introduce each new character

- rhyme, rhythm, and repetitive refrains
- detailed illustrations, with some extra clues in them for observant readers

Getting Inside the Author's Head

First the teacher and the children browse through the book to identify and list the characters and the clues the author and illustrator has provided for each one. They organize this information on a chart showing the characters and a language clue and a picture clue for each. Next, they browse through the book again, this time concentrating on how the story is organized. This helps them decide on the number of characters and events they will need. They brainstorm possible characters, listing language and picture clues they could use.

Characters	Language Clue	Picture Clue
Snow White	It's the dwarfs' lovely friend…	
Humpty Dumpty	Who's that falling off the wall clumpty	wall
	It's my egg friend…	

Innovating on Traditional Tales and Fables

Folktales provide powerful structures for innovation. For emergent and early readers, *The Gingerbread Man* and *The Little Red Hen* can be changed by adding a character, changing all the characters, or changing the setting.

In the following example, Ms. Hopkins and the children in her first-grade classroom have decided to write an innovation on *The Gingerbread Man* by changing the setting. They begin by creating a chart listing the setting for the traditional story, the characters, what they said, and who ate the Gingerbread Man. Ms. Hopkins follows this by reading the children an innovation by Berthe Amoss, *The Cajun Gingerbread Man* (1994). After they have enjoyed this version of the story, they browse through the book again and add details about that innovation under each heading.

Setting	Characters	What They Said	Who Ate Him
A village	Man/woman	STOP! STOP!	Fox
	Boy/girl	STOP! STOP!	
	Dog/cat		
	Fox		
A fishing village	Man/woman	Oh my	Crocodile
	Shrimpers	Bon appetit	
	Fiddler		
	Farmer		
	Crocodile	You look good	
		enough to eat!	

Having established a model for their innovation, the children brainstorm to fill in the details before writing *The New York City Gingerbread Man*.

Setting	Characters	What They Said	Who Ate Him
New York City	Old man	STOP!	Taxi driver
	Old woman	STOP!	
	Flower seller		
	Hot-dog man		
	Dog walker		
	Taxi driver	STOP! STOP! I'll	
		give you a ride!	

Figure 8.2 shows the taxi driver in pursuit of the New York City Gingerbread Man.

Another example, this time of an innovation on a fable, comes from a group of third graders, who have changed the characters from *The Lion and the Mouse* to a cast of native Australian animals, including a dingo and a tiny Sphinex Hopping Mouse, and the setting to the Australian bush.

The story opens with Dingo resting under a tree after devouring a stolen sheep. When Hopping Mouse has the misfortune to hop over Dingo's nose and wake him, Dingo threatens to eat him too. Like the mouse in the original story, Hopping Mouse begs for his life and tells the

Figure 8.2

Dingo that one day he might be able to help him (see Figure 8.3). A look at the pages these children created shows how much thought has gone into not only the setting, plot, and characterization but also into the print size, design, and layout.

Using Informational Books as Models for Writing

Informational texts provide powerful models for writing for different purposes and audiences. By planning, organizing, and communicating their thinking as they read informational texts, students are able to use their ability to find and interpret information as they read other informational texts. Each opportunity to use these texts for shared and guided writing also provides children with models to use in their independent writing.

Begin by covering selected parts of a book and writing new text as a shared writing activity.

Demonstrate how writers think by planning, thinking out loud, and writing in front of the children, involving them in decisions about content, grammar, organization, spelling, and punctuation. As soon as children are able to do some of the writing themselves, have them act as scribes as much as possible.

Adding a New Entry

The following example of an innovation by a second-grade class draws on the language, text structure, organization, and layout of a popular

Dingo was angry. "I'm going to eat you up!" he howled.

One day I will help you." This made the very clever dingo laugh.

"You're too little to help me. You're too little to eat. Go away, you silly mouse, but beware next time we meet" Then one day Dingo got caught in a trap. "Help me! Help me!" howled Dingo. "Who can get me out

of this trap?"

The bush animals heard Dingo howling. They came and looked at him.

"I can't help you," laughed Kookaburra, and away he flew.

"I can't help you," hissed Python," and away she slithered.

"I can't help you," said Red Kangaroo," and away. he jumped.

Figure 8.3

informational book, *Creature Features* (1988) by David Drew. The children decided to add another two-page entry to the book. They began by looking in detail at pictures of their creature before writing the list of characteristics that would provide the clues to its identity.

In this box I've got a creature.
Guess what it is by checking each feature.

How many legs?
4
How many eyes?
2
What's its color?
Green
What's its shape?
Short and squat
What does it feel like?
Slippery and slimy
It must be…

Other Innovations

Other ways to extend informational texts through innovations include the following:

- writing a contents page, index, glossary, or additional glossary entry
- creating headings and subheadings
- adding captions or labels written on Post-it notes
- writing about children's own experiences of the topic and adding it as an appendix
- adding other entries based on the structure of the book
- presenting the information through other graphic forms, such as diagrams, time lines, and charts
- writing questions that could be the basis of further research

9

Choosing Resources for Shared Reading

A reader must develop a self-extending system for himself and to do so requires appropriate texts that are rich in information.

Marie Clay

Shared reading is the driving force of a balanced literacy program. The richness and appropriateness of resources and how effectively they are used by a responsive teacher will largely determine the extent to which children develop a self-extending system in both reading and writing. For these reasons, informed choice of these materials is critical.

Don Holdaway (1979) alerted us to the need for thoughtful choice when he wrote, "The much lauded bedtime story is only half the picture; practice of reading-like behavior and writing-like behavior completes the picture" (p. 61). The texts need to support the development of an integrated network of understandings about written language.

The first books and charts enlarged by Holdaway and his colleagues and used in shared reading were chosen from "the most satisfying children's literature available" (1979, p. 66). They included versions of the traditional tale *The Three Billy Goats Gruff,* which was chosen for "the strongly emotional language of the repetitive section," and *The Gingerbread Man.*

The qualities in these books that made them excellent choices were these:

- a simple, satisfying story line
- a strong, rhythmic quality to the language
- rhyme
- repetition
- action
- a dramatic ending

In addition, the stories were well known to many children in both written and oral versions. Holdaway's selection quickly grew to include well-known songs and poems, which he and his colleagues wrote on large charts.

When big books for shared reading were initially developed in the 1970s, their content and design was informed by a large body of research into literacy learning and teaching and proven teaching strategies. Thus the books were grounded in consistent theory. Careful attention was paid to every detail of their development. Content, concepts, language, print size and placement, layout, and illustrations were orchestrated to ensure that the books would support teaching and learning about reading and writing.

The language in these books was rich and interesting, as were their topics. These resources lent themselves to many revisitings for rereading and exploring written language. They also provided opportunities for art, drama, mime, and dance, and for integration with science and social studies.

As the use of shared books became widespread, many trade children's books were enlarged and promoted as shared reading books. However, while these are often excellent books for reading to children, other than with a few notable exceptions they have neither the content nor the design features of books for reading *with* and *by* children. This has resulted in a great deal of confusion among teachers about the difference between reading aloud and shared reading and their respective roles in a balanced program.

The practice of calling all enlarged texts "big books," although practical, has created the perception that if it is big, it is suitable for shared reading. Unfortunately, this is not always so. Good shared reading materials are purposely built to support the development of reading and writing.

When teachers ask me to help them select shared resources, the first things we consider are how well the children will enjoy and relate to the texts and how well they will be supported and challenged by them. We also consider what purposes they will serve in demonstrating and involving children in reading and writing and how they will support the goals of the classroom program, providing what Holdaway (1979) called "lively examples of the skill in action" (p. 23).

We make sure the books selected for shared reading are within "the zone of proximal development" (Vygotsky 1978). Vygotsky defines the zone of proximal development as the edge of a learner's competence where, although the child is as yet unable to learn independently, they can do so with appropriate adult help. Initially the children will need the support of an experienced reader to model how readers think and read, and to engage them in thinking and acting like readers. As they become familiar with the text and accessing the meaning and content, the children will play an increasingly active role in the reading and their need for scaffolding diminishes. As they develop an understanding about some print features and the different ways written language is organized according to the writer's purpose, they will use this knowledge to predict and confirm, in concert with semantic and syntactic information.

As they tune in to the organization of the texts and the structure and meaning of the language, they begin to recognize and read predictable parts of the books and consistently recognize some high-frequency words. With more experience, the children will need less and less teacher support, and they will be able to read the texts largely independently. In concert with this, the children will begin to generate novel reading responses as they internalize strategic reading behavior.

I also make sure that a variety of text types are represented. In addition, shared reading materials should provide layers of meaning that invite thinking and discussion as well as repeated reading, both shared and independent. The appeal of the topic, the richness and appropriateness of the language, the style and layout of the print and pictures, the potential for innovation, and the relevance of the content and concepts each contribute to the effectiveness of the text.

In the bedtime story situation the opportunity for the child to return to books for practice and further exploration is a powerful source for reinforcement as well as new learning. I strongly believe that in early childhood classrooms it is also vitally important that each teacher or teacher team have their own core collection of shared reading resources that they and the children can return to over the year for reading and rereading, for mini-lessons, and for small-group and individual work.

As Marie Clay (1991) reminds us:

Texts should be continuously available for long periods because they can be revisited by children who are at different levels of independence in dealing with print.

The opportunity for children to return frequently to re-read a wide variety of familiar material allows them to:
- orchestrate the complex patterns of responding to print
- read the books with increasing levels of independence (p. 184)

As demonstrated in the examples in previous chapters of both at-home and classroom reading, every opportunity to revisit a book provides learners with the opportunity not only to confirm and maintain meaning but to generate new meaning. Only when texts are available over an extended period of time in the classroom can children fully benefit from their use in the program.

Familiar books provide a solid foundation of known resources for children who come from homes where reading materials are not readily available. They enable these children to be members of the literacy community in the classroom. The availability of these resources is especially important in classrooms where there are ESL learners. These resources, and in particular those with meaningful, repetitive, and cumulative structures, are memorable. They provide a familiar context for ESL children to revisit English-language patterns and structures and to apply their increasing facility with their new language. With real-world topics about things, places, and events and their use of photographs, informational shared reading materials are also an excellent resource to confirm what children already know while at the same time building additional vocabulary and concepts.

The core collection in each room does not need to be huge or costly. Published and teacher-made posters of songs, rhymes, raps, playground chants, and poetry can be laminated and added to the collection and can also be written on overhead transparencies. Innovations the children themselves have written based on books in the collection are a wonderful addition to the classroom resources and usually become the children's favorites.

The Different Needs of Emergent, Early, and Fluent Readers

Carefully chosen texts play a key role in a child's development as a reader. Although shared resources are selected for a larger group, with varying levels of experience and expertise, they should be chosen with the same care as that used when choosing guided reading books. The needs and interests of the children, the increase in complexity of language and language forms, the structure of the language, the layout and organization of the text, the size and spacing of the print, and the topic all need to be considered in conjunction with the purposes the books will be used for. Above all, the books must delight the children and be worth returning to again and again. They have to stand the test of time.

Children's literacy learning attitudes, understandings, and behaviors can be grouped broadly into three overlapping stages: emergent, early, and fluent (Mooney 1990). As they grow and develop as readers and writers, learners need to experience the satisfaction and success of working with the familiar to practice and consolidate what they know and experience the challenge of working with the new. This lays a solid foundation for literacy learning.

The rest of the chapter describes some of the behaviors and understandings of emergent, early, and fluent readers. It also outlines features to look for in shared texts that will support and ensure continued development.

Emergent Readers

Shared reading can help teach emergent readers to:

- delight in reading
- develop a positive concept of themselves as readers
- think and act like readers and writers
- develop book and print concepts
- develop phonemic awareness
- predict, check, confirm, and self-correct using meaning, structure, and visual information
- use pictures to predict and confirm meaning
- use oral language as a strong cueing system
- consistently recognize and read some high-frequency words
- recognize and use cumulative, repetitive, cultural, and hierarchical patterns and structures to predict

The following table lists the features of supportive text for emergent readers and why each is important.

Feature	Rationale
Clear, readable print style suitable for large-group reading	Facilitates engagement
Ample space between words and lines	Supports one-to-one matching; helps develop concepts of letter and word; enables explicit work with letter clusters and words
Print separated from pictures	Shows difference between pictures and print information; helps children focus on, and clearly see, print details
Some rhyme, rhythm, repetition	Encourages active participation; provides toeholds into text; supports recognition of some high-frequency words
Rich, memorable language	Highlights patterns in the language; develops phonemic awareness; supports active engagement
Some familiar cultural sequences	Relates and builds connections to real-world experiences
Predictable organization	Facilitates engagement and understanding
Inevitability of events	Supports predicting and confirming
Strong, satisfying story line	Ensures active engagement with the text; supports sustained participation
Text that builds momentum to carry the reader forward	Enhances comprehension and fluency; enables instant word recognition
Layout that supports learning and teaching	Supports consistent recognition of text features
Bright, vigorous, supportive illustrations	Enhance meaning; enable cross-checking between pictures and print to predict, confirm, or self-correct; provide context for discussion and attention to detail; support inferencing
Bold, italicized, or other special print features	Draw attention to print, its features, and its meaning

Narrative

The modern classic *Mrs. Wishy-Washy* (Cowley and Melser 1984) is a perfect example of a supportive text for emergent readers. Large, clear illustrations support meaning. One line of large, well-placed print and memorable language carry the story and invite engagement with the print. Children and teachers delight in the humor and energy of the story line and the illustrations, and it is only moments before a chorus of children's voices is bringing life to the repetitive refrain of "wishy washy, wishy washy" as each animal has a turn in Mrs. Wishy-Washy's bathtub. Deceptively simple in appearance, the text provides many opportunities for reading work and innovation.

Over the years I have seen many innovations on this text. My favorite featured a school principal zealously washing all her teachers. The bubbles featured a head-and-shoulders photo of each teacher, who of course in the end turned the tables on the principal.

The language and structure of *Crunchy Munchy* (Parkes 1997) features a similar kind of rhythm to *Mrs. Wishy-Washy*. A strong, repetitive refrain moves the story along:

In went horse.
Crunchy Munchy,
Crunchy Munchy.
In went cow.
Crunchy Munchy,
Crunchy Munchy.

Bright, lively illustrations support meaning making. The print and layout are easy to follow. The book also features strong characterizations in Farmer Rosie and her animals as they vie for the ripe red apples in her orchard. The layout and language in this book also provide many opportunities for reading work and practice with high-frequency words.

Brown Bear, Brown Bear (Martin 1983) is another well-loved classic that has earned its place in the hearts and minds of teachers around the world. This text introduces children to a cumulative repetitive structure that builds prediction and confirming strategies. The large, clear illustrations and simple story line support reading and lend themselves to innovation.

Farmer Schnuck (Parkes 1992) has large, clear print with ample spacing between words and a consistent layout. This book provides plenty of action throughout and a humorous ending. It also includes positional language, such as *over, through, past,* and *down,* which is well supported by the strong illustrations. Children delight in the animals' response to Farmer Schnuck's invitation to rejoin him on the ride.

The Enormous Watermelon (Parkes 1986) is based on the structure of The Tale of the Turnip and features a cast of nursery rhyme characters who come to help Mother Hubbard harvest an enormous watermelon. Split pages provide strong picture clues for children to predict who each character will be before they turn the page to confirm their prediction by checking the illustrations and print. This helps children learn to scan print and illustrations, predict, and check before confirming or self-correcting.

The Goat in the Chile Patch (Kratky 1989) is sure to become a favorite. The layout is excellent and the language and illustrations engaging. Children love the humor, the inviting language, and the satisfying story line and revel in the repetitive chant

But oh! Uh oh! The goat was not the one to go!

They become totally involved as the wily old goat returns over and over again to feast in the chile patch, managing to dispatch all comers until he himself is dispatched by a tiny ant.

The engaging language and illustrations support a good deal of mime and dramatization as the story line unfolds, which is a great support to ESL learners.

The Gingerbread Man (Parkes and Smith 1986), *The Little Red Hen* (Parkes 1985), *The Three Billy Goats Gruff* (Smith and Parkes 1989), and *Goldilocks and the Three Bears* (Hillman 1989) are traditional tales that are good choices for emergent readers. These retellings provide special features, such as bold, enlarged print to highlight dramatic parts of the story and colored print for dialogue. Careful formatting places repeated phrases directly in line, which draws children's attention to repetitive refrains, cumulative text, and action, thus encouraging reading and discussion.

Nonfiction

David Drew's books for early science are new classics for nonfiction reading. For emergent readers, the following titles are especially appropriate.

What Did You Eat Today? (Drew 1998c) is a good choice for introducing young readers to nonfiction text. This highly interactive book presents simple graphs as children follow the daily food intake of a number of zoo animals. It also encourages children to ask and seek answers to questions.

Creature Features (Drew 1988) provides a powerful model for children's own writing through a consistent layout. It also draws children's attention to the importance of noticing detail in pictures, and sets up a cycle of predicting, checking, and confirming or self-correcting from language and picture clues.

I Spy (Drew 1998b) prompts children to predict and confirm from repetitive descriptions and picture clues. It also provides letter-sound clues to help identify each creature—for example:

> What can it be?
> It starts with V.

This supports predicting, checking, and confirmation or self-correction using semantic, syntactic, and graphophonic information.

Amazing Eggs (Llewellyn 1998) from the Discovery World series, is an excellent book to support the idea of looking for details in photographs. It also demonstrates the use of labels. This book has a clear, consistent layout that supports prediction.

Legs (Theodorou 1998), also from the Discovery World series, is a good choice for showing children how to read and write labels. It shares the photographic and layout features of *Amazing Eggs*.

Poetry

Of course no collection of shared reading resources for emergent readers would be complete without songs, rhymes, and poems. These are excellent materials for developing phonemic awareness. I get one anthology with a representative collection and accompanying audiotape and single copies of other books. A useful anthology is Bookshop Stage 1: Songs and Rhymes, Charts and Cassette. Shelley Harwayne's *Jewels: Children's Play Rhymes* (Greenvale, NY: Mondo, 1995) is another good choice. This collection features rhymes from many different countries.

Some Good Books for Emergent Readers

Annotations

Cowley, J., and J. Melser. 1984. *Mrs. Wishy-Washy*. Bothell, WA:
Wright Group.

Jorgensen, G. 1988. *Crocodile Beat*. Crystal Lake, IL: Rigby.

Kratky, L. J. 1989. *The Goat in the Chile Patch*. Carmel, CA: Hampton
Brown.

Martin, B. 1983. *Brown Bear, Brown Bear*. New York: Henry Holt.

Parkes, B. 1986. *The Enormous Watermelon*. Crystal Lake, IL: Rigby.

———. 1992. *Farmer Schnuck*. Columbus, OH: SRA McGraw Hill.

———. 1997. *Crunchy Munchy*. Greenvale, NY: Mondo.

Traditional Tales

Hillman, J. 1989. *Goldilocks and the Three Bears*. Crystal Lake, IL: Rigby.

Parkes, B. 1986b. *The Little Red Hen*. Crystal Lake, IL: Rigby.

Parkes, B., and J. Smith. 1986. *The Gingerbread Man*. Crystal Lake, IL:
Rigby.

Smith, J., and B. Parkes. 1989. *The Three Billy Goats Gruff*. Crystal
Lake, IL: Rigby.

Nonfiction

Drew, D. 1988a. *Creature Features*. Crystal Lake, IL: Rigby.

———. 1988b. *I Spy*. Crystal Lake, IL: Rigby.

———. 1988c. *What Did You Eat Today?* Crystal Lake, IL: Rigby.

Llewellyn, C. 1998. *Amazing Eggs*. Crystal Lake, IL: Rigby.

Theodorou, R. 1998. *Legs*. Crystal Lake, IL: Rigby.

Further Choices

Narrative

Ada, A. F. 1993. *Bears Walk*. Carmel, CA: Hampton Brown.

Buxton, J. 1994. *Snap! Splash!* Huntington Beach, CA: Pacific Learning.

Cowley, J. 1988. *Greedy Cat Is Hungry*. Huntington Beach, CA: Pacific
Learning.

———. 1996. *The Little Yellow Chick*. Bothell, WA: Wright Group.

———. 1998a. *The Hungry Giant*. Bothell, WA: Wright Group.

———. 1998b. *The Meanies*. Bothell, WA: Wright Group.

Davison, A. 1988. *The Lion and the Mouse*. Crystal Lake, IL: Rigby.

Goss, J. L., and J. Harste. 1995. *It Didn't Frighten Me*. Greenvale, NY:
Mondo.

Green, R., and B. Scarfe. 1992. *Starting School.* Columbus, OH: SRA McGraw Hill.

Heo, Y. 1994. *One Afternoon.* New York: Orchard Books.

Jorgeson, G. 1988a. *Beware.* Crystal Lake, IL: Rigby.

———. 1988b. *One Dark and Scary Night.* Crystal Lake, IL. Rigby.

Morris, A. 1995. *Shoes, Shoes, Shoes.* New York: Lothrop, Lee & Shepard.

Parkes, B. 1989. *The Fox and the Little Red Hen.* Melbourne: Oxford University Press.

———. 1992a. *Farmer Schnuck.* Columbus, OH: SRA McGraw Hill.

———. 1992b. *One Foggy Night.* Columbus, OH: SRA McGraw Hill.

Vaughn, M. 1995. *Hands, Hands, Hands.* Greenvale, NY: Mondo.

Nonfiction

Berger, M. 1992. *Squirrels All Year Long.* New York: Newbridge.

———. 1994. *Growing Pumpkins.* New York: Newbridge.

———. 1995. *The Four Seasons.* New York: Newbridge.

———. 1996. *Sounds of the Farm.* New York: Newbridge.

Coad, P. 1992. *Goodnight.* Columbus, OH: SRA McGraw Hill.

Drew, D. 1992. *Make a Pizza Face.* Columbus, OH: SRA McGraw Hill.

Ray, S., and K. Murdoch. 1992. *Just Right for the Night.* Columbus, OH: SRA McGraw Hill.

Early Readers

Shared reading at the early level supports children to build on their emergent reading ability. It also helps them:

- maintain meaning over extended pieces of text
- build momentum over longer texts
- work on phrasing
- self-monitor
- cross-check information
- integrate meaning, structural, and visual cues
- use multiple sources of information
- rely less on pictures and use more information in print
- notice details and draw inferences from picture cues
- know some frequently used words automatically

For early readers the features of supportive text for emergent learners are still important. Additional features for this group include the following.

Feature	Rationale
Language- and information-rich texts	Allow readers to draw on all cue systems to make meaning; provides redundancy; adds to predictability
Logical organization	Enhances processing
A range of genres	Engages readers with different forms and functions of written language; causes readers to set purposes and choose method of reading
Illustrations that support, extend, and confirm meaning	Enhance inferencing; encourage readers to search for detail and connections
Language and layout that supports phrasing	Enhances fluent, phrased reading; supports instant recognition of words
Multilayered texts	Make possible a variety of problem-solving skills, strategies, and behaviors

Narrative

A Farm's Not a Farm (Parkes 1989a) features a double-page spread of a farm scene without animals, then a double-page spread of a marketplace where a farmer and his wife have gone to buy animals. This sets the children up to use the farm scene first to predict what animals they need, then to use this information as they make choices from the market. The title invites innovation; *A School's Not a School; A Zoo's Not a Zoo; A Supermarket's Not a Supermarket* are some very effective examples I have seen.

Goodnight, Goodnight (Parkes 1989b) helps children orchestrate cue systems by drawing meaning from multiple sources of information. The layout of this text is designed to lead children through the predicting-checking-confirming cycle using picture clues, rhyming clues, print clues, and semantic information about the characters.

When the King Rides By (Mahy 1986) has wonderful rhythm and lyrical language that engages and carries readers along. The hilarious illustrations capture the fun of the crowd scenes and keep children involved and interested over many readings. This is an excellent resource to model searching for detail in illustrations and to build fluency and phrasing over many rereadings.

Who's in the Shed? (Parkes 1986) has rhyme, rhythm, and repetition. The layout and design of the print support the development of fluent, phrased reading. In addition, the book has a special feature: peepholes cut into the pages. These peepholes invite readers to use cumulative picture clues to predict who is in the shed, making it possible for all the children to be involved in meaning making from the outset. Redundancy in the language makes this an ideal book to demonstrate written cloze.

Chicken Little (Hillman 1989) is retold against a background of superb collage pictures that bring the characters to life. This engaging version of the old favorite is enhanced by some clever highlighting of action words, which supports meaning and draws attention to the visual features of print.

Jack and the Beanstalk (Smith and Parkes 1986) features a range of print treatments to highlight dramatic parts of the story and engage readers with the text. This story lends itself to dramatization and mime.

Puss in Boots (Hillman 1990) uses different-color print to highlight dialogue. The repetitive layout supports prediction. It also helps readers gain and maintain momentum that supports instant recognition of words and fluent, phrased reading.

The Three Little Pigs (Smith and Parkes 1984) is a vibrant retelling of this old favorite. The illustrations are lively and strongly portray characterization. Each character's dialogue is written in a different-color print, providing excellent support for part reading and dramatization. Careful attention to design and layout provides a framework for work with words.

The Three Little Pigs: A Play (Parkes 1997) provides the opportunity to introduce play reading through a well-known story. The character parts are shaded in light watercolor to help children easily recognize when it is their turn.

Nonfiction

How Animals Move (Byrne 1998) is an excellent introduction to nonfiction text featuring well-written content and accessible design. Each animal is discussed using the same headings across a double-page spread. The book also features a chart that compares how different animals move.

Looking at Insects (Glover 1998) is another excellent nonfiction example from the same series as *How Animals Move.* The layout, design, and organization are simple and clear and provide powerful models for reading and writing. Labeled diagrams further enhance the usefulness of the book, and questions that prompt children to look closely at details in the illustrations help them maintain a high interest level.

Poetry

Kaufman, W., ed. 1991. *Catch Me the Moon, Daddy.* Crystal Lake, IL:
    Rigby.

Some Good Books for Early Readers

Annotations
Mahy, M. 1986. *When the King Rides By.* Greenvale, NY: Mondo.
Parkes, B. 1986. *Who's in the Shed?* Crystal Lake, IL: Rigby.
———. 1989a. *A Farm's Not a Farm.* Crystal Lake, IL: Rigby.
———. 1989b. *Goodnight, Goodnight.* Crystal Lake, IL: Rigby.

Traditional Tales
Hillman, J. 1989. *Chicken Little.* Crystal Lake, IL: Rigby.
———. 1990. *Puss in Boots.* Crystal Lake, IL: Rigby.
Parkes, B. 1997. *The Three Little Pigs: A Play.* Crystal Lake, IL: Rigby.
Smith, J., and B. Parkes. 1984. *The Three Little Pigs.* Crystal Lake, IL:
    Rigby.
———. 1986. *Jack and the Beanstalk.* Crystal Lake, IL: Rigby.

Nonfiction
Byrne, D. 1998. *How Animals Move.* Crystal Lake, IL: Rigby.
Glover, D. 1998. *Looking at Insects.* Crystal Lake, IL: Rigby.

Further Choices

Poetry (Songs and Plays)

Baskwill, J. 1996. *Somewhere*. Greenvale, NY: Mondo.

Teberski, S. 1996. *Morning, Noon, and Night*. Greenvale, NY: Mondo.

Narrative

Ada, A. F. 1993. *Giraffe's Sad Tale*. Carmel, CA: Hampton Brown.

Borg, P. 1996. *The Greedy Goat: A Traditional Tale*. Greenvale, NY: Mondo.

Cowley, J. 1988a. *The Sandwich That Max Made*. Crystal Lake, IL: Rigby.

———. 1988b. *The Springtime Rock and Roll*. Crystal Lake, IL: Rigby.

Dixon Lake, M. 1996. *The Royal Drum: An Ashanti Tale*. Greenvale, NY: Mondo.

George, S. 1992. *Bad Dog, George!* Columbus, OH: SRA McGraw Hill.

Kratsky, L. J. 1992. *In a Faraway Forest*. Carmel, CA: Hampton Brown.

Pollock, Y. 1994. *The Old Man's Mitten*. Greenvale, NY: Mondo.

Smith, J., and B. Parkes. 1984. *The Ugly Duckling*. Crystal Lake, IL: Rigby.

Nonfiction

Berger, M. 1993a. *Animals in Hiding*. New York: Newbridge.

———. 1993b. *A Butterfly Is Born*. New York: Newbridge.

———. 1994. *Big Bears*. New York: Newbridge.

Cullen, E. 1996. *Spiders*. Greenvale, NY: Mondo.

Drew, D. 1987a. *Animal Clues*. Crystal Lake, IL: Rigby.

———. 1987b. *The Life of a Butterfly*. Crystal Lake, IL: Rigby.

———. 1987c. *Tadpole Diary*. Crystal Lake, IL: Rigby.

———. 1992. *How Many Legs?* Columbus, OH: SRA McGraw Hill.

———. 1992. *Something Silver, Something Blue*. Columbus, OH: SRA McGraw Hill.

Freeman, M. 1999a. *A Bird's-Eye View*. Pelham, NY: Benchmark.

———. 1999b. *Where Do You Live?* Pelham, NY: Benchmark.

———. 1999c. *Young Geographers*. Pelham, NY: Benchmark.

Green, R. 1996. *Caterpillars*. Greenvale, NY: Mondo.

Llewellyn, C. 1995. *Amazing Eggs*. Crystal Lake, IL: Rigby.

Ray, S., and K. Murdoch. 1992. *Snake*. Columbus, OH: SRA McGraw Hill.

Ray, S., and K. Murdoch. 1992. *The Ant Nest*. Columbus, OH: SRA McGraw Hill.

Fluent Readers

Supportive text for fluent readers provides practice in known strategies and challenges them to:

- read with ease and appropriate phrasing
- read a variety of print styles and layouts
- maintain meaning over longer texts
- interpret and analyze complex texts
- set purposes for reading
- work with a range of text types
- draw inferences
- learn to interpret and use pictures, diagrams, charts, and tables
- change their way of reading to suit their purpose
- read a wide range of texts for different purposes

Features of supportive text for fluent readers, along with the reasons for them, are as follows:

Feature	Rationale
A range of text types	Enables exploration of the writer's craft
Appropriate language and writing style for the text type	Supports prediction based on knowledge of language and text structures
A balance between print and visuals	Helps students recognize and read visual literacy
Considerate placement of print and visuals	Helps students access information and see connections between the information in visual and written text
Humor	Engages thinking and enhances enjoyment

Narrative

Rumpelstiltskin (Parkes 1990) is useful in extending children's experiences with traditional tales. The language and layout support the development of fluent, phrased reading. The increasingly sophisticated language, such as the words *astonished, astounded,* and *amazed* (used to describe how the king feels as the miller's daughter turns straw to gold), supports discussion and word work.

Whale Rap (Von Bramer and Scott 1992) combines two different text types or genres, rap and informational text, on facing pages. This makes the book a powerful resource to demonstrate how readers should shift their approach depending on the type of material they are reading and their purpose for reading it.

The Wolf's Story (Parkes 1999) is another example of a rap. The fast-moving, humorous text tells the story of the Three Little Pigs from the perspective of the wolf. Character references for the wolf are supplied by a shifty cast, including Pinocchio, Snow White's stepmother, and the wolf's mother. This book provides many models and invitations for children's own writing.

Why Flies Buzz (Parkes 1992) and *Why Frog and Snake Can't Be Friends* (Davidson 1992) provide experience with traditional stories from West Africa. Both books offer rich opportunities for higher-level thinking and the exploration of language.

Nonfiction

Investigating Your Backyard (Lunis 1999), from the Thinking Like a Scientist series, is a powerful resource for teaching about the way nonfiction text is structured to support comprehension of photographs, diagrams, and specialized language.

Going to the City (Freeman 1999), from the People, Spaces and Places series, provides a useful model for reading in the content area of social studies with a focus on directional and positional language. The book includes simple maps as well as a contents page and an index.

Blast Off with Ellen Ochoa (Gonzalez-Jensen and Rillero 1999), from the Greetings series, is an engaging introduction to reading and writing biography, told through a question-and-answer format. In addition, the book features short informative captions.

The Cat on the Chimney (Drew 1992), from the Realizations series, is an excellent resource to help children learn how to use information from pictures and diagrams. Each double-page spread details a problem on the left-hand page, with a variety of items and information on the facing page that can be used to reach a solution to the problem. This clever series is perfect for teaching inferences as well as critical and higher-order thinking.

Thinking About Ants (Brenner 1997) is a sophisticated information book told in verse in a question-and-answer format. It provides a powerful model for children to consider information in relation to themselves. The book also introduces the use of cutaway diagrams. Clear, detailed illustrations throughout provide a useful resource for children's learning how to write captions and labels.

Homes and Living (Freeman 1999) integrates labels, captions, and running text with photographs, line drawings, and cutaways. This is a useful book to show children how this information works in concert.

Some Good Books for Fluent Readers

Annotations
Von Bramer, J., and J. Scott. 1992. *Whale Rap*. Crystal Lake, IL: Rigby.

Traditional Tales
Davidson, A. 1992. *Why Frog and Snake Can't Be Friends*. Crystal Lake, IL: Rigby.
Parkes, B. 1990. *Rumplestiltskin*. Crystal Lake, IL: Rigby.
———. 1992. *Why Flies Buzz*. Crystal Lake, IL: Rigby.
———. 1999. *The Wolf's Story*. Crystal Lake, IL: Rigby.

Nonfiction
Brenner, B. 1997. *Thinking About Ants*. Greenvale, NY: Mondo.
Drew, D. 1992. *The Cat on the Chimney*. Crystal Lake, IL: Rigby.
Freeman, M. 1999a. *Going to the City*. Pelham, NY: Benchmark.
———. 1999b. *Homes and Living*. Pelham, NY: Benchmark.
Gonzalez-Jensen, M., and P. Rillero. 1999. *Blast Off with Ellen Ochoa*. Crystal Lake, IL: Rigby.
Lunis, N. 1999. *Investigating Your Backyard*. New York: Newbridge.
Theodorou, R. 1998. *Prehistoric Record Breakers*. Crystal Lake, IL: Rigby.

Further Choices

Poetry

DeCoteau Orie, S. 1995. *Did You Hear the Wind Sing Your Name?*
Greenvale, NY: Mondo.

Cullinan, Bernice, ed. 1996. *A Jar of Tiny Stars.* Urbana, IL: National
Council of Teachers of English.

Narrative

Aldridge, R. 1992. *I Remember When.* Columbus, OH: SRA McGraw
Hill.

Cartright, P. 1991. *The Fisherman and His Wife.* Crystal Lake, IL: Rigby.

Nonfiction

Bourne, P. M. 1992. *Things Change.* Carmel, CA: Hampton Brown.

Freeman, M. 1999. *Coast to Coast.* Pelham, NY: Benchmark.

Hart, T. 1992. *Antarctic Diary.* Columbus, OH: SRA McGraw Hill.

Moore, H. 1996. *Beavers.* Greenvale, NY: Mondo.

Quinn, P. 1994. *Bumble Bee.* Glenview, IL: Celebration Press.

General Guidelines

Some questions that I find helpful to guide myself in choosing shared
reading resources include the following:

- Will the children I teach find this resource challenging, interesting, and appealing?
- Does it have the substance and high interest level to invite many rereadings for many purposes?
- In what ways do the size, spacing, and placement of the print support the reader?
- Are the language and language style appropriate?
- Is the text organization logical?
- Do the pictures support the written text?
- Do the pictures extend the written text?
- Do the pictures invite children to search for details?
- Are there a variety of styles in the pictures?
- Do the language and language structure invite innovation?

- Does the text reflect the genre in language, structure, and organizational features?
- If a nonfiction book, does it have a range of organizational features, including a contents page, headings, an index, labels, captions, and a glossary?
- If a nonfiction book, does it have visuals, including maps, diagrams, and labeled drawings?

Used in conjunction with informed kidwatching, shared reading has the power to develop self-extending readers who believe in themselves as learners and who love to read. In our daily teaching with these resources, if we, the teachers, keep in mind the spirit conveyed in the words of Don Holdaway, that "learning to read and write ought to be one of the most joyful and successful of human undertakings" (1979, p. 11), we can make these words come true for the learners whose lives we touch.

Who's in the Shed?
The Author's Perspective

When I write shared books I have a dual agenda. On the one hand I am writing for children; on the other, I am writing for teachers.

For the children, my first priority is to delight them in the book and in the reading. I also invite them to participate actively in meaning making in many different ways. In addition, I want to encourage them to believe in themselves as readers and build the capacity to be self-extending learners. As I write, I constantly imagine how the children will think; how they will respond to different parts of the language and illustrations; where they will first find their way into the book; the text features they will notice and talk about; the rhythm of their voices as they read together and bring the book to life; and the looks on their faces as they successfully solve problems.

Pacing is everything. I try to ensure a balance between pages that require the children to do some solid reading work and pages where they can luxuriate in some repetitive text. Line and page breaks that support fluent, phrased reading; repetitive print that aligns so that it "pops out" and helps the children recognize the constancy of written language; expressive language written in print that matches its sound; colored print to identify dialogue. All of these are an integral part of the writing.

If I get it right for children, there is every chance that it will be right for teachers as well. Each of the above features supports teaching as well as learning. In addition to using large print, I try to select print fonts that are plain and easy to see and to ensure that the illustrations do not obscure the print. Ample spacing between words and lines is critical to support masking, framing, word and line matching, and other word work.

It is also important to line up rhyming words, or group words in close proximity to each other to support explicit teaching. It is not serendipitous that the words "'How dare you stare!' roared the circus bear" appear on a two-page spread in *Who's in the Shed?* The text is deliberately crafted to set up possibilities for explicit teaching about *dare*, *stare*, and *bear* if and when it is warranted. The dialogue bubbles that enclose the conversation between McBungle and his wife in *McBungle Down Under* (Parkes 1987) make each person's speech overt and sets up a teaching opportunity for direct speech.

The following analysis of *Who's in the Shed?* illustrates how this dual agenda operates. The front cover (below left) shows all the characters, with of course the exception of the mysterious character in the shed. The cover illustration and title provide a framework for discussion about who the characters are, the sound each one makes, and why they might be looking so worried.

The first page (below right) provides a clue that the story takes place at night, and shows that the animals are very startled. Key concepts are established at the outset.

Pages 2 and 3 (above), a double-page spread, presents the whole cast again, this time looking toward a shed. A truck with the word *circus* written on the side is backed up to the shed. The truck provides a powerful opportunity for assessment, as the children who notice and understand the written clue will be predicting circus characters, while others will be predicting more globally. The text layout thus far highlights rhyming words (*night* and *fright*; *led* and *shed*) as well as word patterns (*howling, growling, roaring, clawing*).

Initially, this layout and language supports thinking, inferring, and participation in the reading. Later, it supports explicit word work. The word *terrible* is written in a bolder print as a signal for the children to read it with emphasis.

The repetitive text on page 3—

"Who's in the shed?"
everyone said.
"Who's in the shed?"

—serves a number of purposes. It shows that the same words in print are constant. The second "Who's in the shed?" allows the more experienced reader to read with confidence and expression and the less experienced

reader to join in. The repetitive lines also support work with matching strips, one-to-one correspondence, and punctuation.

The text on page 4 (above)—

"Let me have a peep,"
baaed the big white sheep.
"Let me have a peep."

—supports all the teaching and learning possibilities discussed in relation to the repetitive text on page 3. In addition to this, the word *baaed* provides a further source of prediction as well as redundancy for the second line of text. It helps those children who know which animal makes that sound predict the word *sheep*. The illustration supports the meaning of the words *big* and *white*. *Sheep* also rhymes with *peep* on the line above it. During shared reading the teacher can use oral cloze to have the children predict and supply the word *sheep*. When the book is later used for explicit teaching, the teacher can use written cloze and cover either the word *sheep* or the word *baaed* and have the children use these multiple sources of information to predict and confirm or self-correct. In later work with written cloze, the words *big* and *white* can be covered and the children can substitute other words, such as *large* and *woolly*, which have a similar meaning and sound right in the context of the text.

Page 5 introduces a repetitive refrain:

So the sheep had a peep
through a hole in the shed.
What did she see?

The refrain is repeated on pages 5, 7, 9, 11, and 13, with only a one-word change for the featured animal's name.

The rhyme and syncopated rhythm of the language support participation. The question "speaks to the reader," inviting a personal response as the children predict who's in the shed from the cutaway picture clue. The "she" on the last line is a deliberate choice. By covering the *s*, the word becomes *he* and provides a simple innovation.

Pages 4, 6, 8, 10, and 12 each feature a different animal. The placement of text remains constant to allow children to use the pattern as a source of prediction and support for the word changes on each of these pages.

"My turn now,"
mooed the sleek brown cow.
"My turn now."

"Let me see in there,"
neighed the old gray mare.
"Let me see in there."

"What is it then?"
clucked the little red hen.
"What is it then?"

"It's something big,"
grunted the fat pink pig.
"It's something big."

The repetition of each animal's dialogue supports participation in the reading by all members of the group.

Each page provides the teacher with a number of opportunities to strategically use oral and written cloze.

The cutaway holes on the facing pages provide clues as to the identity of the creature in the shed. Children are encouraged to change their minds or validate their predictions as they examine each new piece of information. This feature was built into the book so that every child in the group could be involved in the thinking, discussion, and meaning making.

Finally, pages 14 and 15 (next page) draw the story to a dramatic climax. The huge print in the speech bubble demands big voices! The large, clear illustration invites discussion about the clues. *Dare, stare,* and *bear* await word work at an opportune time.

On page 16 (next page), the last page of the story, the print runs away, as do the animals. The open-ended conclusion invites discussion and, of course, the writing of another episode.

Nonfiction Series

S everal nonfiction series are published by various firms. Publishers' addresses and lists of their series follow.

Newbridge Educational Publishing
333 East 38th Street
New York, NY: 10016

Thinking Like a Scientist Series
Lumis, N., and N. White. 1999. *Investigating Your Backyard.*
———. 1999. *Being A Scientist.*
———. 1999. *Bugs All Around.*
———. 1999. *A Closer Look.*
———. 1999. *Investigating Rocks.*
Thompson, G. 1999. *Kitchen Science.*
———. 1999. *Let's Experiment.*
Randolph, J. A. 1999. *Science Tools.*
———. 1999. *A World of Change.*

Early Science Series
Berger, M. 1992. *Squirrels All Year Long.*
———. 1993. *Animals in Hiding.*
———. 1993. *A Butterfly Is Born.*
———. 1993. *See, Hear, Touch, Taste, Smell.*
———. 1994. *Growing Pumpkins.*

———. 1995. *Busy as a Bee.*
———. 1995. *The Four Seasons.*
———. 1996. *Animals and Their Babies.*
———. 1996. *Where Do the Animals Live?*
———. 1996. *The World of Ants.*
———. 1998. *What Is a Cycle?*

Nature's Diversity Set
Cory, C. 1998. *The Rain Forest.*
Freeman, M. 1998. *Wetlands.*
Lunis, N. 1998. *Rocks and Soil.*
Trumbauer, L. 1998. *Follow the River.*
———. 1998. *What Is a Cycle?*

Rand McNally
Skokie, IL 60076

People, Spaces, and Places Series
Freeman, M. 1999. *A Bird's Eye View.*
———. 1999. *Coast to Coast.*
———. 1999. *Going to the City.*
———. 1999. *Where Do You Live?*
———. 1999. *Young Geographers.*
Wicklander, C. 1999. *What Changes Our Earth?*

Rigby Education
P.O. Box 797
Crystal Lake, IL 60039

Series Informazing
Drew, D. 1987. *Animal Clues.*
———. 1987. *The Book of Animal Records.*
———. 1987. *Caterpillar Diary.*
———. 1987. *Mystery Monsters.*
———. 1987. *Tadpole Diary.*
———. 1988. *Creature Features.*
———. 1988. *Hidden Animals.*

———. 1988. *Somewhere in the Universe.*
———. 1988. *What Did You Eat Today?*
———. 1989. *The Life of a Butterfly.*
———. 1990. *I Spy.*

Realization
Drew, D. 1992. *Which Habitat?*
———. 1992. *What Should I Use?*
———. 1993. *Clever Island.*

Discovery World
Byrne, D. 1998. *How Animals Move.*
Flint, D. 1998. *Our Book of Maps.*
———. 1998. *What Is a Park?*
———. 1998. *Where Does Breakfast Come From?*
Gibbs, B. 1998. *All Kinds of Eyes.*
Glover, D. 1998. *Looking at Insects.*
Hughes, M. 1998. *Seasons.*
Powell, J. 1998. *Sizes.*
Theodorou, R. 1998. *Legs.*

References

Adams, M. 1995. *Beginning to Read: Thinking and Learning About Print.*
  7th ed. Cambridge, MA: MIT Press.
Amoss, B. 1994. *The Cajun Gingerbread Man.* New York: Hyperion.
Armbruster, B., J. Anderson, M. Armstrong, C. Janisch, and L. Meyer.
  1991. Reading and Questioning in Content Area Lessons. *Journal of
  Reading Behavior* 23: 35–59.
Askew, B., and I. Fountas. 1998. "Building an Early Reading Process:
  Active from the Start!" *The Reading Teacher* 52: 126–134.
Bacon, R. 1997. *Jessie's Flower.* Auckland, NZ: Shortland.
Baghban, M. 1984. *Our Daughter Learns to Read and Write: A Case Study
  from Birth to Three.* Newark, DE: International Reading
  Association.
———. 1996. *As Big as a Whale.* New York: Newbridge.
Cambourne, B. 1998. *The Whole Story: Natural Learning and the
  Acquisition of Literacy in the Classroom.* New York: Ashton Scholastic.
Carle, E. 1969. *The Very Hungry Caterpillar.* New York: Putnam.
Chappell Carr, J. 1999. *A Child Went Forth: Reflective Teaching with
  Young Readers and Writers.* Portsmouth, NH: Heinemann.
Clay, M. 1991. *Becoming Literate: The Construction of Inner Control.*
  Portsmouth, NH: Heinemann.
———. 1998. *By Different Paths to Common Outcomes.* Portland, ME:
  Stenhouse.
Cochran-Smith, M. 1984. *The Making of a Reader.* Norwood, NJ: Ablex.
Cory, C. 1998. *The Rain Forest.* New York: Newbridge.
Cowley, J., and J. Melser. 1984. *Mrs. Wishy-Washy.* Bothell, WA:
  Wright Group.
Doake, D. 1981. "Book Experience and Emergent Reading in
  Preschool Children." Ph.D. diss., University of Alberta.

Dombey, H. 1983. "Learning the Language of Books." In M. Meek, ed., *Opening Moves*. London: Bedford Way Papers.

Dorn, L. J., C. French, and T. Jones. 1998. *Apprenticeship in Literacy: Transitions Across Reading and Writing*. Portland, ME: Stenhouse.

Drew, D. 1988. *Creature Features*. Crystal Lake, IL: Rigby.

Duthie, C. 1996. *True Stories: Nonfiction Literacy in the Primary Classroom*. Portland, ME: Stenhouse.

Eggleton, J. 1997. *Rat-a-tat-tat*. Auckland, NZ: Shortland.

Fountas, I. C., and G. S. Pinnell. 1998. *Word Matters: Teaching Phonics and Spelling in the Reading/Writing Classroom*. Portsmouth, NH: Heinemann.

Glover, D. 1998. *Looking at Insects*. Crystal Lake, IL: Rigby.

Goss, J., and J. Harste. 1995. *It Didn't Frighten Me*. Greenvale, NY: Mondo.

Goswami, U., and P. Bryant. 1990. *Phonological Skills and Learning to Read*. Hillsdale, NJ: Lawrence Erlbaum.

Greene, R., Y. Pollock, and B. Scarfe. 1995. *When Goldilocks Went to the House of the Bears*. Greenvale, NY: Mondo.

Hansen, J. 1987. *When Writers Read*. Portsmouth, NH: Heinemann.

Heath, S. B. 1982. "What No Bedtime Story Means: Narrative Skills at Home and School." *Language in Society* 11: 49–76.

Hill, E. 1980. *Where's Spot?* New York: Putnam.

Holdaway, D. 1979. *The Foundations of Literacy*. Portsmouth, NH: Heinemann.

Hoyt, L. 1999. *Revisit, Reflect, Retell: Strategies for Improving Reading Comprehension*. Portsmouth, NH: Heinemann.

Hutchins, P. 1968. *Rosie's Walk*. New York: Macmillan.

International Reading Association and National Association for the Education of Young Children (joint statement). 1998. "Learning to Read and Write: Developmentally Appropriate Practices for Young Children." *The Reading Teacher* 52: 193–213.

Keene, E. O., and S. Zimmermann. 1997. *Mosaic of Thought: Teaching Comprehension in a Reader's Workshop*. Portsmouth, NH: Heinemann.

Kratky, L. 1989. *The Goat in the Chile Patch*. Carmel, CA: Hampton Brown.

Llewellyn, C. 1998. *Amazing Eggs*. Crystal Lake, IL: Rigby.

London, J. 1993. *Voices of the Wild*. New York: Crown.

Lunis, N. 1999a. *Investigating Your Backyard*. New York: Newbridge

———. 1999b. *A Closer Look*. New York: Newbridge.

Lunis, N., and N. White. 1999. *Bugs All Around.* New York: Newbridge.

Martinez, M., and N. Roser. 1985. "Read It Again: The Value of Repeated Reading During Storytime." *The Reading Teacher* 38: 782–786.

Meek, M. 1996. *Information and Book Learning.* Stroud, UK: Thimble Press.

Mooney, M. 1990. *Reading To, With, and By Children.* New York: Richard C. Owen Publishers.

Moore, H. 1996. *Beavers.* Greenvale, NY: Mondo.

Moustafa, M. 1997. *Beyond Traditional Phonics: Research Discoveries and Reading Instruction.* Portsmouth, NH: Heinemann.

———. 1999. "Whole-to-Part Phonics Instruction: Building on What Children Know to Help Them Know More." *The Reading Teacher* 52: 451.

Parkes, B. 1985. *The Little Red Hen.* Crystal Lake, IL: Rigby.

———. 1986. *Who's in the Shed?* Crystal Lake, IL: Rigby.

———. 1987. *McBungle Down Under.* Crystal Lake, IL: Rigby.

———. 1989a. *The Fox and the Little Red Hen.* Melbourne, AU: Oxford University Press.

———. 1989b. *Goodnight, Goodnight.* Crystal Lake, IL: Rigby.

———. 1990a. "Explorations of Emergent Literacy Learners' Transactions with Picture Storybooks." Ph.D. diss., University of Wollongong.

———. 1990b. *The Royal Dinner.* Crystal Lake, IL: Rigby.

Parkes, B., and J. Smith. 1986a. *The Gingerbread Man.* Crystal Lake, IL: Rigby.

———. 1986b. *The Three Little Pigs.* Crystal Lake, IL: Rigby.

Pearson, P. D., and L. Fielding. 1991. "Comprehension Instruction." In R. Barr, M. L. Kamil, P. Mosenthal, and P. D. Pearson, eds. *Handbook of Reading Research.* New York: Longman.

Pinnell, G. S., and I. C. Fountas. 1996. *Guided Reading: Good First Teaching for All Children.* Portsmouth, NH: Heinemann.

———. 1998. *Word Matters: Teaching Phonics and Spelling in the Reading/Writing Classroom.* Portsmouth, NH: Heinemann.

Richgels, D., K. Poremba, and L. McGee. 1996. "Kindergarteners Talk About Print: Phonemic Awareness in Meaningful Contexts." *The Reading Teacher* 49: 632–642.

Smith, J., and B. Parkes. 1988. *The Three Billy Goats Gruff.* Crystal Lake, IL: Rigby.

Sulzby, E. 1985. "Children's Emergent Reading of Favorite Storybooks: A Developmental Study." *Reading Research Quarterley* 20, 458–481.

Tolstoy, A. 1968. *The Great Big Enormous Turnip.* New York: Franklin Watts.

Vaughan, M. 1995. *Hands, Hands, Hands.* Greenvale, NY: Mondo.

———. 1997. *Crocodile Tea.* Auckland, NZ: Shortland.

Vygotsky, L. 1962. *Thought and Language.* Cambridge, MA: MIT Press.

———. 1978. *Mind in Society.* Cambridge, MA: MIT Press.

Wallace, K. 1994. *Red Fox.* Cambridge, MA: Candlewick.

Walpole, S. 1999. "Changing Texts, Changing Thinking: Comprehension Demands of New Science Textbooks." *The Reading Teacher* 52: 357–370.

Yaden, D. 1988. "Understanding Stories Through Repeated Read Alouds: How Many Does It Take?" *The Reading Teacher* 41: 556-560.

Zion, G. 1956. *Harry the Dirty Dog.* New York: HarperCollins.